Seasons

Cross-Curriculum Units
for Theme Teaching

Written by Patricia O'Brien

Edited by Nan Ryan

Illustrated by Darcy Tom

Teaching & Learning Company

1204 Buchanan St., P.O. Box 10
Carthage, IL 62321-0010

Cover by Darcy Tom

Copyright © 1997, Teaching & Learning Company

ISBN No. 1-57310-075-7

Printing No. 98765432

Teaching & Learning Company
1204 Buchanan St., P.O. Box 10
Carthage, IL 62321-0010

FALL

WINTER

This book belongs to

_____

SPRING

SUMMER

Table of Contents

Summer 73

The Seasons 97

Dear Teacher or Parent,

As the Earth rotates around the sun each year, we experience the four seasons. Because the Earth tilts on its axis, the Northern Hemisphere is toward the sun in the summer and away from it in the winter. It is the opposite in the Southern Hemisphere, when July is a winter month and January is warm.

During the summer, the sun is higher in the sky. More of the sun's heat and light reach us during the longer daylight hours. In winter, the sun is lower in the sky. It rises later and sets earlier. The weather is colder because we receive less of the sun's energy.

Spring and autumn fall between the extremes of summer and winter. In spring, the Earth comes back to life, as it gradually warms. In autumn, the days slowly grow cooler and people, plants and animals prepare for the coming winter.

Those who live in the tropics do not have four seasons. The rays of the sun strike the area directly. The temperature varies slightly, but they may experience wet and dry seasons. Desert areas have little rainfall. Jungles have rain year round.

This book of seasons is designed to be used as a resource and idea book for educators in the primary grades. Background information is presented for each season. Questions to spark interest are included. Activities to develop critical and creative thinking are indicated. Suggestions have been made to extend lessons and connect classroom experiences with real-life situations.

Sincerely,

Pat

Patricia O'Brien

Fall

Do You Know?

Why do leaves change color in the fall?

How do animals get ready for winter?

How do people prepare for the changing weather?

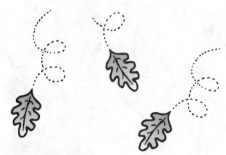

Teacher Background

The autumnal equinox, on September 21 or 22, marks the beginning of the new season. Night and day are of equal length. The harvest moon, the first full moon of autumn, appears low on the horizon and resembles a giant pumpkin. Seasonal pollen and smoke in the air account for its orange color.

Changes occur as nature begins to shut down to survive the coming frost. Life-giving sap retreats to the roots of deciduous trees. Chlorophyll is no longer produced by the leaves. Colors, once masked by the green pigment, begin to appear. Leaves of brilliant hues drop from the branches.

Animals hurry to prepare for winter. They store food, eat everything in sight or get ready for a long migration to warmer climates. Some insects also migrate. Their trip may be underground below the frost line.

Migrating birds fly great distances and return to the same place at the start of spring. Some scientists believe they use the sun and stars to navigate. Others think they are influenced by the Earth's magnetic field. Whatever it is, birds often fly hundreds of miles with extraordinary accuracy.

Information

Summer is over. Autumn has begun. As the days grow shorter and cooler, farmers pick the last of the apples, pears and nuts from the trees. Animals collect food for the winter or eat their fill in preparation for a long rest. Squirrels scurry to gather nuts to store for the cold winter months when food will be scarce.

Trees get ready for the approaching cold weather. Leaves, once green, turn yellow, red and orange. They flutter to the ground where they crunch underfoot. They slowly turn brown and crumble, returning to the soil.

Overhead, birds can be seen and heard heading south for warmer weather and a better food supply. Ducks and geese leave before the ponds freeze.

Seeds travel, too. Some are taken by the wind. Others stick to animal's fur and are carried away. It is too cold for seeds to grow, so they wait, protected by their coverings, for the warmer days of spring.

Where do insects go when it gets cold? Some lay eggs before they die. The eggs will be sheltered until the warm weather returns. Caterpillars spin cocoons and, hidden from sight, slowly change into butterflies. Bees stay in their hives eating honey they have stored. Beetles migrate deeper into the ground.

Talk About

How can you tell fall has arrived?

What do you like best about this season? What do you dislike?

── Words to Know ──

deciduous   evaporation   hibernation   migration   rain

Use the reproducible on page 21 to reinforce these vocabulary words.

Weather Watch

☐ Rain

Water vapor rises, cools and turns into cloud-forming droplets. When these drops of water bump against each other, they join to make bigger drops. These heavier drops fall as rain.

Discovery Experiences

☐ Water Droplets

To show students how water droplets join together, have them do the following activity. They will need waxed paper, a toothpick, one drinking straw for each group and water.

Give each student a piece of waxed paper and a toothpick. Have them place a few drops of water on the waxed paper with the straw. Direct them to push the drops gently with the toothpicks, so they bump against each other. What do they notice when two drops touch?

Making a Connection

Ask the students to write or tell about the experiment. They should explain what they did and what happened. Can they explain the connection to rain falling?

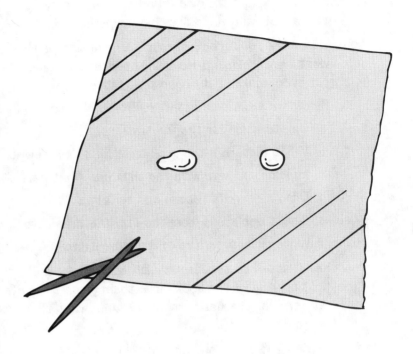

☐ Evaporation at Work

On a rainy day, when it stops raining and the sun comes out, pick a puddle where the class can observe evaporation. With their help, draw a chalk line around the outside edge of the puddle. Depending on how warm the sun is, check the puddle every 30 to 45 minutes. As the puddle evaporates, draw additional lines to outline its shrinking size. Record the time when each new line is drawn.

Making a Connection

Ask the children what they think happened to the water in the puddle. Discuss how the heat of the sun turns the water into vapor that we cannot see. The vapor rises into the sky to form clouds. Repeat the activity on another day that has more or less wind. Compare the two activities. Explain that wind also causes evaporation. Clothes hung on a line will dry more quickly if the wind is blowing on a sunny day.

Additional Activities

1. Can you explain how the water in a puddle becomes a rain shower?
2. Draw a picture showing an ocean, lake or pond, the sun, clouds and rain.

Read and Enjoy

1. *Rain*, by Peter Spiers, is a classic wordless picture book that tells the adventure of two children as they explore their neighborhood on a rainy day. Before "reading" the story, have the children talk about rainy days they have experienced.

   Share the book in small groups. The first time through, talk about what the two children see and what they are doing. Have the students imagine what the children might be saying to each other. Let them make up dialogue that fits each scene.

   Below are additional activities from which to choose.

   a. Create titles for the illustrations.

   b. Pick a picture in the book to think, talk and write about.

   c. Imagine you were with the children. What part did you like best?

   d. Draw a rainy day scene and tell about it.

   e. Select one scene from the story to dramatize.

   f. Write or dictate a rainy day adventure.

2. Read *Listen to the Rain*, by Bill Martin, Jr., and John Archambault to the children. During the first reading of the book, have them close their eyes and listen to the sounds of the changing rainstorms. Discuss with the children what they imagined as they listened to the words of the story.

   Reread the story showing the illustrations. With the students help, make a list of words and phrases that describe the sounds of rain.

   a. Draw a picture that shows one phrase from the list.

   b. Draw a two-part picture to show a quiet rain and a noisy storm.

   c. Using just your fingers to tap on the desktop, demonstrate the different sounds of rain.

Additional Activities

Materials
classified section
felt-tipped markers
crayons
scissors
glue
12" x 18" (30 x 46 cm) paper

Directions

1. Have the students create a rainy day city scene.

   a. Cut out different-sized buildings from the newspaper. They can follow the column lines to make tall, short, narrow and wide buildings.

   b. Glue the shapes in place on the paper, overlapping structures. Use a black pen or crayon to outline the buildings and windows.

   c. Cut clouds from the newspaper and glue them above the city.

   d. Colored markers may be used to add people hurrying along the sidewalks and cars in the street.

10   Fall

2. A rainbow appears after a shower when the sun comes out and there is still water in the air. As the sun passes through the droplets, the rays are separated into bands of color. All rainbows are red, orange, yellow, green, blue, indigo and violet, from top to bottom.

    a. Use watercolors to paint a rainbow on a large sheet of paper.

    b. Select a writing suggestion from below.

- Explain how rainbows form.

- Compose a rainbow poem. Begin each line with a color name.

- Write a story about the pot of gold that is supposed to be at the end of the rainbow.

3. Talk to the children about where animals go when it rains. What animals would not mind getting wet? Read *Where Does the Butterfly Go When It Rains?*, by May Garelick. Ask the children where they think butterflies go to keep dry.

Plants
☐ Harvest Time

Pumpkins ripen in fall. They have grown all summer and are now ready to be turned into jack-o'-lanterns and pumpkin pies.

Activities

Using pumpkins in the classroom provides opportunities to estimate, weigh, count, cook and paint.

1. Have the children guess how much the pumpkin weighs. Record the estimates. Discuss ways to find the exact weight. Weigh the pumpkin and compare the results with the estimates. Repeat this activity with another person. This should produce more realistic estimates.

2. Carve the lid from the top of the pumpkin. Let the children see the seeds inside and guess how many there are. Scoop out the seeds, rinse them and count them together. In small groups, the children can take turns counting the seeds by 2s, 5s and 10s.

3. Remove the seeds from the second pumpkin for roasting. Wash the seeds in warm water and spread them to dry on a paper towel. In a bowl mix 2 cups (480 ml) of seeds with 1 tablespoon (15 ml) of vegetable oil and 1 teaspoon (5 ml) of salt. Bake in a 250°F (120°C) oven for 30 minutes. Turn with a spatula two or three times. The pumpkin seeds are ready to eat as soon as they cool.

4. Use miniature pumpkins for the following activities:

    a. Have the children paint faces on the pumpkins. Provide poster paints and felt-tipped pens.

    b. Compile a class big book of jack-o'-lanterns. Have the students paint pictures of scary, friendly or unusual jack-o'-lanterns.

5. Read *The Biggest Pumpkin Ever*, by Steven Kroll.

    a. What steps did the two mice take to grow a very large pumpkin?

    b. Discuss how both their dreams came true because they cooperated.

Special Feature
☐ Scarecrows

Scarecrows are placed in fields and gardens to keep crows and other birds from ruining the growing plants. They seldom scare the crows or the other hungry birds. The unusual scarecrows in the poem, on page 22, however, probably did scare the farmer.

1. Hand out copies of the poem. Read it aloud and discuss the following questions with the students:

    a. What do you think the farmer said when he found the scarecrows here, there and everywhere?

    b. Why do you suppose the scarecrows are dancing?

2. Divide the class into small groups to illustrate the poem. Each student in the group may draw a picture to interpret one stanza.

3. Present the poem as a choral reading. Display the illustrations during the performance.

12   Fall

Trees

☐ Color Change

Deciduous trees shut down as the days of fall grow cooler. Sap returns to the roots. When the leaves stop producing chlorophyll, they turn from green to red, yellow and orange. Then they fall to the ground.

1st Drawing

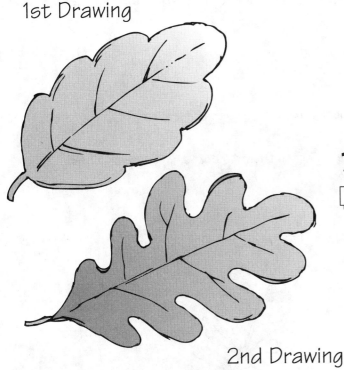

2nd Drawing

Discovery Experience

☐ Leaves

Have the students do a pencil drawing of a leaf. They should include everything they can remember about it. When they have completed their work, pass out a variety of leaves for them to study. How do their drawings compare to the real leaves? Direct the students to make a second drawing with a leaf model in front of them. Then compare their two sketches commenting on how they differ.

I used to think leaves _____.

Now I know they _____.

Special Feature

☐ Leaves

Note: Leaves that are collected for study and art projects should be pressed to preserve them. Put them between sheets of newspaper and place heavy books on top to flatten them overnight.

1. Take the children on a field trip to a park or on a walk through the neighborhood. Along the way, have them pick up at least 10 different kinds of leaves. Can they find the types of trees the leaves came from?

2. Watch the leaves fluttering from the branches. Notice how they float and spin to the ground. Think of words to tell how they fall. After returning to the classroom, brainstorm a list of words that describes the movements of the leaves from limb to landing.

3. Combine art and poetry to make stained glass windows.

   a. Help the students arrange pressed leaves between folded sheets of plastic wrap. When they are satisfied with the arrangement, they may smooth the wrap with their hands to seal in the leaves.

   b. Have the students compose a poem about leaves, using the list prepared in #2 for ideas.

      Example: Leaves

               Fluttering, floating

               Twisting, turning,

               Down to the ground.

   c. The final draft should be written on construction paper. Attach the leaves above the poem in a paper frame.

4. Have the children study their collection of leaves. Direct them to sort the leaves by shape. Ask them what other ways the leaves may be grouped.

Leaf Art

1. Make a rubbing to show the shape of the leaf with the veins running through it.

   Directions:

   a. Place a leaf vein-side up on a cleared work space.

   b. Cover with a lightweight sheet of paper.

   c. Color with the side of a crayon until the outline of the leaf appears.

2. Make an aluminum foil leaf rubbing. Each student will need a leaf, a piece of cardboard a little larger than the leaf and heavy-duty aluminum foil a little longer than the cardboard.

   Directions:

   a. Use a drop of glue to hold the leaf in place on the cardboard.

   b. Cover with the foil, wrapping it around the edges.

   c. Crayons may be used on the foil to highlight parts of the leaf.

3. The veins of some leaves resemble the limbs of trees. A single leaf looks like a very small tree. Make a forest scene on paper using leaves for trees. Before gluing the leaves in place, use crayons or pencils to color in the background.

14   Fall

Fall Apple Trees

In the fall, the apple crops are gathered. The biggest apples are carefully picked by hand. Smaller, less well-formed apples, are used for juice, cider and applesauce. Machines shake these fruits from the tree. They are gathered and taken to processing plants.

There are many varieties of apples from which to choose. Some are best eaten as they come off the tree. Other kinds make delicious pies, sauce or juice. Most are placed in cold storage and are available at markets throughout the year.

Determine if any students have ever visited an orchard, picked apples or had any other firsthand experience. If apples are grown in the area, discuss the types that are found nearby. What kinds are sold at the local market?

 # Cooking Connection

Applesauce

Make applesauce with the children. After the apples are peeled and cored, plastic knives may be used to cut them into smaller chunks. Combine the apples and water in saucepan. Bring to a boil over medium heat. Lower the temperature and simmer until the apples are tender. Stir in sugar and nutmeg and cook one minute longer. The variety of apple used will determine the amount of sugar needed. Variation: Make two batches of sauce using two kinds of apples, or use the same apples but omit the sugar from one.

Conduct an applesauce taste test. Give everyone two small servings in paper cups to compare. Have the children tell which one they liked better and why they preferred it.

Make a list of ways apples may be prepared (applesauce, juice, baked, pie, candied or caramel apple). Conduct a survey to determine how the members of the class like their apples. Display the result on a bulletin board bar graph. Distribute 2" (5 cm) squares of paper—one to each child. Have them draw an apple on the square. Set up a bar graph on the bulletin board. Invite the students to select their favorite by placing their apple square on the graph.

Special Feature

☐ Johnny Appleseed

John Chapman (b. 1774–d. 1847), known as Johnny Appleseed, wandered the countryside planting apple seeds. He made friends with the Indians and the settlers moving west.

1. Select a story about Johnny Appleseed to read to the class. Mention that some of his deeds were probably imaginary. After his death, the legend continued to grow.

2. To review and summarize, discuss and list events from the story. The students may use the list to complete one of the following activities:

   a. Pick one item to illustrate.

   b. Fold a sheet of paper into fourths. In each section, draw a picture to show scenes from Johnny Appleseed's life.

   c. Select facts to write in chronological order (the order in which they happened).

3. People often keep a journal to remind themselves of things that happened. Have the children imagine that they lived in olden times, when Johnny was alive. He is spending a few days with them, helping with chores and planting apple seeds. Direct the students to write three journal entries telling about Johnny's stay with the family.

4. Have the students imagine what it would be like to travel with Johnny. If they were there, what would they like to ask him? How would he probably answer their questions?

5. Use the responses from the above activity to develop a lesson on questions and answers. Point out the words that are often used to begin questions—*who, when, why, where, what, how, do, did* and *can*. Note the question mark used to punctuate a sentence that asks a question.

6. To reinforce asking and answering techniques, distribute copies of page 23 to the students. Have them follow the directions to complete the page.

7. Celebrate Johnny Appleseed's birthday on September 26 with apple treats. Plan to share apple juice and slices of apple. Chopped apples may be added to cupcake or cookie batter.

8. Have the students use crayons or felt-tipped pens to decorate place mats. They may make apple designs to form a border around a sheet of construction paper.

Insects

☐ Ants

Read *Those Amazing Ants*, by Patricia Brennan Demuth, or a similar book that tells about the habits of the ant.

Since it would be difficult for a large group to follow an ant trail, suggest an independent study of ants.

Where to find them:

> near an anthill
>
> close to a food source
>
> at a picnic

What to observe:

> how small insects move large loads
>
> how they "talk" to one another
>
> how they work together

Place cookie, bread or cracker crumbs near the ant trail. How long does it take them to find the food? Which do they seem to prefer?

Read *Two Bad Ants*, by Chris Van Allsburg. Review the story by asking the students the following questions:

1. What dangers did the ants face on their way to gather crystals?
2. Why did two ants stay behind, when the others returned home?
3. What adventures did the two ants have?
4. Which was the most frightening?

Birds

☐ Migration

In the fall, many birds prepare to fly south to warmer weather. Ducks and geese, who live in ponds and lakes, leave before the water freezes. Other birds head south to find food. They stop along the way to rest and feed.

Activities

1. Talk about migrating birds with the children. Have they noticed V-shaped formations in the skies as flocks pass overhead? If they live in a warmer climate they may see new birds arriving.

2. Read *Round Robin*, by Jack Kent. Unlike other birds, Round Robin was too round to fly. He began walking south. On the way he learned firsthand why the other robins flew south to avoid the snow. Do you think he learned a lesson?

Animals
☐ Hibernation/Migration/Adaptation

Animals are on the move in the fall. As the days shorten and grow cooler, the search for food is endless. Squirrels store nuts for a winter food supply. Deer who climbed high into the mountains to feed in the summer migrate down where the snow is not as deep and food is available. Chipmunks eat and grow fat. They will hibernate underground during the cold months.

Cold-blooded animals like frogs and snakes also hibernate. Their body temperature changes with their surroundings. They are unable to stay warm, so they go underground. Below the frost line they are protected from the cold under a blanket of snow.

1. Discuss with the students why animals hibernate and migrate. Explain that some animals, especially in milder climates, are able to adapt to seasonal changes. While less food is available, they are less active and do not use as much energy.

2. Hand out page 24. Assign one of the following activities according to the age and ability of the students.

   a. Color and cut apart the pictures at the bottom of the page. Decide to which category each belongs. Glue the pictures under the correct heading.

   b. Use the pictures to illustrate a booklet explaining how plants and animals survive the winter.

   c. Write a report about one of the animals pictured in each group. Use the drawings to illustrate your report.

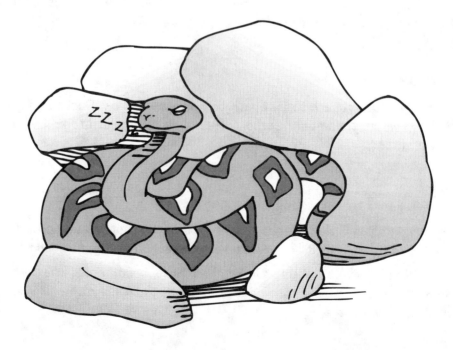

18   Fall

Read and Enjoy

1. Have the students imagine what it would feel like to be a small animal preparing for the winter snows. What would they have to do to get ready? Read *Chipmunk Song*, by Joanne Ryder to get a better idea how animals prepare to hibernate.

2. Unlike chipmunks, mice store extra food but do not hibernate.

   Read *Frederick*, by Leo Lionni. While the other field mice worked to store food for the winter, Frederick gathered sun rays, colors and words. As winter progressed and the food supply dwindled, Frederick shared the memories he had collected.

   a. Take the class on a mini field trip to gather colors and words for an autumn poem. Compose a haiku. The 17 syllables are arranged in three unrhymed lines (5-7-5). Young children can clap out the sounds even if they don't know about syllables.

   Example:

   > Leaves fall quietly
   >
   > twisting, turning through the air
   >
   > dropping to the ground.

   b. Present *Frederick* as a puppet play. Create stick puppets of the mice based on illustrations from the book. Help the students make up dialogue to fit the action. What might the mice be saying to each other as they gather food for the winter? Combine invented dialogue with direct quotations from the book.

People

People are busy in the fall, too. It's time to put away summer clothes and take out warmer ones. There are leaves to rake and firewood to pile to prepare for colder days and nights. Farmers harvest the last of the crops. Apples, nuts, corn and grapes are gathered. Pumpkins will be picked and used for pies, soups and jack-o'-lanterns.

Signs of Fall

To summarize what was presented about fall, hand out copies of pages 25 and 26. Direct the students to illustrate each section. They may then cut along the lines and staple the pages together to make a booklet. More pages may be included as the children think of additional signs of the season.

Resources

Nonfiction

Demuth, Patricia Brennan. *Those Amazing Ants.* New York: Macmillan Publishing Company, 1994.

Garelick, May. *Where Does the Butterfly Go When It Rains?* Reading, MA: Addison-Wesley, 1961.

Hirschi, Ron. *Fall.* New York: Cobblehill Books, 1991.

Maass, Robert. *When Autumn Comes.* New York: Henry Holt and Company, 1990.

Maestro, Betsy. *Who Do Leaves Change Colors?* New York: HarperCollins Publishers, 1994.

Markle, Sandra. *Exploring Autumn.* New York: Atheneum, 1991.

Martin, Jr., Bill, and John Archambault. *Listen to the Rain.* New York: Holt, 1988.

Ryder, Joanne. *Chipmunk Song.* New York: Lodestar Books, 1987.

Simon, Seymour. *Autumn Across America.* New York: Hyperion Books for Children, 1993.

Sohi, Morteza. *Look What I Did with a Leaf!* New York: Walker and Company, 1993.

Spiers, Peter. *Rain.* Garden City, New York: Doubleday, 1982.

Whitlock, Ralph. *Autumn.* New York: The Bookwright Press, 1987.

Fiction

Aliki. *They Story of Johnny Appleseed.* Englewood Cliffs, NJ: Prentice-Hall, Inc., 1963.

Kellogg, Steven. *Johnny Appleseed.* New York: Thomas Y. Crowell, 1986.

Kent, Jack. *Round Robin.* Englewood Cliffs, NJ: Prentice-Hall, Inc., 1982.

Kroll, Steven. *The Biggest Pumpkin Ever.* New York: Holiday House, 1984.

Lionni, Leo. *Frederick.* New York: Pantheon, 1967.

Slawson, Michele Benoit. *Apple Picking Time.* New York: Crown Publishing, Inc., 1994.

Van Allsburg, Chris. *Two Bad Ants.* Boston: Houghton Mifflin Company, 1988.

Fall Vocabulary Match

Draw a line connecting each word with the correct picture.
Color the pictures.

deciduous

migration

hibernation

rain

evaporation

The Scarecrow

When the moon is full
When the little mice prance
When the farmer sleeps
The scarecrows dance.

They stomp and kick
It's quite a sight
They twirl and spin
All through the night.

When morning comes
When skies are light
When the farmer awakens
And views the sight.

The scarecrows are smiling
With wide-eyed delight
And straw is scattered
To the left and the right.

The scarecrows sigh
In the bright sunlight
"We'll dance no more,
But, then, we might!"

TLC10075 Copyright © Teaching & Learning Company, Carthage, IL 62321-0010

Name _____

Questions and Answers

Match the question in Column A with the correct answer in Column B.

Column A

1. What made Johnny Appleseed happiest?
2. Where did Johnny get the seeds to plant?
3. Why weren't the wild animals afraid of Johnny?

Column B

1. He collected seeds from the cider mills.
2. They trusted him to be kind.
3. Many apples grew.

Write a question. Begin each sentence with the words given below.

1. Who _____

_____

2. When _____

_____

3. Why _____

_____

The answer is Johnny Appleseed. What is the question? Write three questions that could be answered by the name *Johnny Appleseed*. Example: *Who planted many apple trees?*

1. _____

2. _____

3. _____

Migrate	Hibernate	Adapt

Name _____

Signs of Fall

Leaves fall from the trees.

Seeds are scattered.

Insects are gone until spring.

Squirrels collect nuts and acorns.

Ducks and geese fly south.

Fall Clip Art

Fall Clip Art

Fall Clip Art

Fall Clip Art

Winter

Do You Know?

Where do animals go in the winter?

Where are the insects in the winter?

Teacher Background

The winter solstice marks the first day of winter. The shortest day of the year occurs on or about December 21. The Northern Hemisphere slants farthest away from the sun.

Storms bring rain and snow. Snowflakes are tiny crystals of frozen water. Ice forms on lakes and ponds. Icicles hang from roofs and tree branches.

Birds have migrated to warmer climates. Cold-blooded animals like snakes and frogs have burrowed below the frost line to survive. They cannot regulate their own temperatures.

Groundhogs and chipmunks hibernate for the winter. They endure freezing weather because they are able to slow their metabolism. Their temperature drops, their heartbeat and breathing are slowed. Very little energy is used. Some animals like raccoons and bears don't hibernate, but go into a deep sleep. They may wake from time to time to eat and then go back to sleep again.

In mild climates animals neither migrate or hibernate. They remain active, adapting to the cooler weather and dwindling food supply. They spend more time resting and do not need as much food to supply energy.

Most plants shut down for the winter. Evergreens, unlike deciduous trees, keep their leaves year round. These cone-bearing trees have tiny needle-like leaves. Their waxy covering protects them from the winter cold.

Information

You can tell it is winter when the days are shorter and the nights are longer. The days are cold and the nights are colder. You can tell it is winter when trees which were once leafy have bare branches. Flowers do not bloom. Bees do not fly. Frogs are nowhere to be seen.

Often there is snow on the ground. In some places snow falls all winter long. In other places it seldom snows. In some parts of the world where it never snows, people have to travel to another area to find snow for sledding and skiing.

About

What are some signs of winter?

What do you like best about winter? What do you dislike?

— Words to Know —

evergreen   icicles   snowflake

Use the reproducible on page 42 to reinforce these vocabulary words.

Weather Watch

☐ Snow

Snow is made of tiny crystals of frozen water. When the weather is cold, snow falls instead of rain. In winter it covers the ground like a blanket. Animals who have gone underground for the winter are protected from icy winds. Plant roots and seeds are safe below the ground until spring.

Unlike raindrops that can be heard as they splatter against the windows, snowflakes land without a sound. During a blizzard or heavy snowstorm, the winds may howl, but the flakes still land softly.

Activities

1. Snowflakes have six sides. No two have been found that are exactly alike. Provide various shaped pasta for the children to use to create original six-sided flakes. They may glue the finished snowflakes on sheets of dark construction paper.

2. Show the children how to make paper snowflakes. Give them lightweight paper and circle templates to use for tracing. After the circles are cut out, direct them to fold the circle in half and then into thirds. Show them how to snip along the edges to create lacy snowflakes.

Note: Coffee filters make good snowflakes. Art tissue paper makes colorful snowflakes.

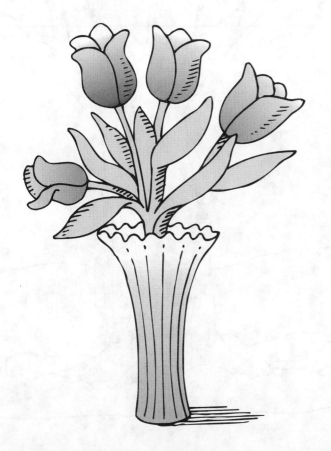

Plants

Plants have different ways of protecting themselves during the cold season. Some plants die when the snow comes, but they leave seeds behind that sprout in the spring. New plants will grow.

Other plants look dead, but down below the surface their roots are protected. In the spring new stems and leaves will grow from the old roots.

Daffodil, tulip and iris bulbs are planted in the fall. They won't start to grow until warmer weather returns in the spring.

1. Read and discuss page 43 with the students. Explain how different types of plants survive the cold winter.

2. Have them complete the page by drawing pictures to show three ways plants survive snowy winters.

Trees

Deciduous trees are bare during the winter. They shed their leaves in the fall. Evergreen trees are built to resist snow and ice. Instead of broad leaves, they have waxy needles that retain water. Snow slides off their sloping branches. Firs, pines and spruces are the most common evergreens.

Activities

Use the crayon resist technique to produce a snow scene. The area that is colored will resist the paint, giving the appearance of falling snow. A thick layer of crayon combined with a thin coat of paint will give the best results.

Materials
paper
crayons
thinned white tempera paint

Directions

1. Create an outdoor scene. Include dark evergreens.
2. Color the picture, pressing hard with the crayons. Dark colors show up best.
3. Apply a thin coat of white paint over the entire paper.

Special Feature
☐ Winter Apple Trees

To survive, apple trees shut down for the winter. Life-giving sap returns underground to the roots. The apple trees have bare branches. There are no leaves, blossoms or fruit. You might think the tree is dead, but it is only resting. The buds that will produce flowers and leaves in the spring need this quiet time to prepare for the season ahead. As spring approaches, the warming temperature makes the sap rise. It flows up through the trunk to the branches and buds.

Have the children draw a picture of an apple tree in winter. Remind them it looks very bare without leaves or fruit.

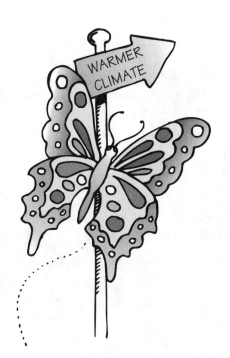

Insects

Insects have numerous ways to survive the winter. Many die as the weather grows cooler, but they lay eggs that will hatch in the spring. Ants dig deeper into the ground and huddle together. Bees form in a ball around their queen. They constantly push and move to get to the warm center. Some butterflies migrate to warmer climates. Mosquitoes and houseflies hibernate in sheltered places.

Activities

Have the students divide their papers in half and draw a two-part picture. On one side they should show insects busy in summer. On the other, show the insects surviving the winter cold.

Birds

Not all birds migrate in the fall. Birds in year-round mild climates stay at home. They have ways of keeping warm when it turns cool. When you go out on a cold day, you might put on a down jacket to keep warm. Birds have to fluff up their feathers. This traps the air around their bodies. You can think of them as wearing little down suits that are lightweight and warm.

You can learn from birds. You don't have feathers to fluff, but you can trap air between thin layers of clothing. It will keep you warmer than one thick layer.

Bird Feeding Station

Birds that don't migrate need some help during the leaner winter months. Set up a feeding station. If possible, place it so the birds can be observed from a classroom window.

Different varieties of birds eat different types of food. A bird-watcher could tell you what the local bird population will enjoy. You could also experiment with an assortment of seeds, corn and suet to see what attracts them. Remember, once you start feeding birds, they will depend on you to continue until their regular food is once again available.

Animals

Migrating animals have left for warmer climates. Hibernating animals sleep deeply through the winter. Their temperature drops. Their heart beat and breathing slow down. The animals that stay active adapt to snowy conditions. If the climate is mild, animals stay where they are and adapt to a dwindling food supply.

Activities

1. To understand how woodland animals adjust to the snows of winter, read *North Country Night*, by Daniel San Souci. Working in groups or independently, have the students learn more about one of the animals mentioned in the story. How is it able to adapt to survive the months of cold?

2. Read and discuss page 44. Explain how animals survive the winter months. Instruct the students to complete the page by drawing pictures to illustrate each section.

3. Plan an animals-in-winter mural. Assign one animal to each small group or individual student. Have them show how their animal spends the winter. To avoid confusion, complete the artwork elsewhere and add it to the mural piece by piece.

4. Sing the following song to the tune of "Are You Sleeping, Brother John."

1. Are you sleeping,
   Are you sleeping,
   Little seed, little seed?
   Safe from the cold winter.
   Safe from the cold winter.
   Spring's not here.
   Spring's not here.

2. Are you sleeping,
   Are you sleeping,
   Little squirrel, little squirrel?
   Stay inside your warm nest.
   Stay inside your warm nest.
   Spring will come.
   Spring will come.

3. Are you sleeping,
   Are you sleeping,
   Little frog, little frog?
   Ice and snow are melting.
   Ice and snow are melting.
   Spring is near.
   Spring is near.

4. Are you hungry,
   Are you hungry,
   Grumpy bear, grumpy bear?
   Time to get some breakfast.
   Time to get some breakfast.
   Spring is here!
   Spring is here!

36   Winter

Literature Connection

The Mitten, A Ukrainian folktale, adapted and illustrated, by Jan Brett.

Summary

One by one the forest animals squeezed into a mitten to get warm. The mitten stretched to accommodate each newcomer. The tiniest visitor, a mouse, made the bear sneeze sending all the animals out into the cold again.

Reading the Story

Read and enjoy the story together. Be sure the children have the opportunity to study the illustrated side panels. They can follow the boy's adventures and preview the next animal to climb into the mitten.

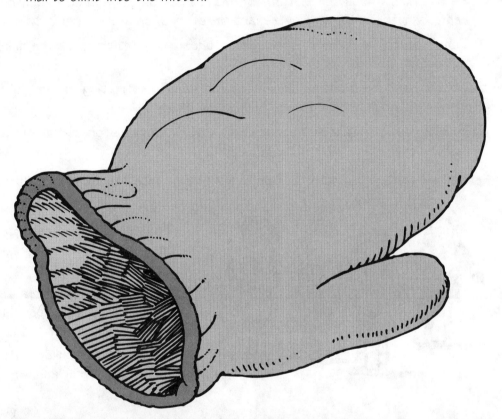

Thinking About the Story

1. What two things will Nicki's grandmother check when he returns home?

2. How many of the animals that squeezed into the mitten can you name?

3. What did you like best about the boy's grandmother?

4. Discuss the following questions with the students. Record the best answer to each question on sentence strips and place them in a pocket chart. Help the students arrange them in chronological order.

   a. What took place when the bear sneezed?

   b. What happened after the boy returned home?

   c. What occurred when the badger spotted the mitten?

   d. What happened when Nicki dropped his mitten?

   Have the students compose additional questions to answer. The responses may be added to complete the story summary on the chart.

Activities

1. Discuss scenes from the story. Have the children select their favorites to display in dioramas.

2. To complete a mobile of the animal story characters, each student will need: copies of page 45, crayons, construction paper, yarn and scissors. A stapler will be needed to connect the yarn to the mitten and animals.

   Direct the students to:

   a. Color and cut out the animal pictures.

   b. On construction paper, trace their hands to make an outline of a mitten.

   c. Staple eight lengths of yarn to the mitten.

   d. Staple the animals to the other ends.

3. As a variation, use the pictures to make stick puppets. Place each on a tongue depressor. The students may reenact the story or create an original tale of their own.

4. Distribute copies of page 46 to each student. Have them name the animals in the riddles and write a riddle of their own.

5. While the animals piled into the mitten, Nicki was investigating the area. After studying the pictures, tell about one thing he did or saw.

6. Imagine you could take Nicki's place in the story. Write a story about your adventures.

Read aloud and enjoy another version of the tale as retold by Alvin Tresselt.

1. Look at the illustrations. Discuss how the animals were portrayed in both books.

2. Assign parts to be read aloud as a reader's theater presentation.

3. After reading both versions of the tale, have the children decide which story they prefer and why.

4. Use a Venn diagram to show the animals in both tales. Help the students compare the characters in the stories. Draw two overlapping circles on the board or chart. Label one *Brett* and the other *Tresselt*.

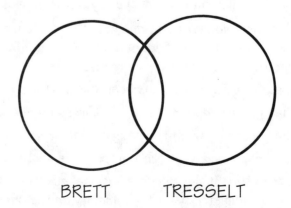

BRETT   TRESSELT

People

In the winter, people dress in extra layers of clothing when they go outdoors. If the snow is heavy, it is harder to get from place to place. There are different types of jobs to be done. Just as plants and animals adjust to winter, people also have to make changes.

1. Make a list of winter jobs, types of work that are only done when it is snowing.

2. Make a list of games that can be played outside during the winter.

3. Have the students work in small groups to invent a new game to play outdoors.

   a. Decide the object of the game. What does one have to do to win? For example, in Tic-Tac-Toe, one has to get three Xs or Os in a row.

   b. Make up some rules but not too many. In Tic-Tac-Toe, the players take turns starting, or whoever won the previous game begins.

Read and Enjoy

1. Read *The Snowy Day*, by Ezra Jack Keats. Peter explores his city neighborhood. Use the following questions to talk about the story and to give the students opportunities to share similar personal experiences.

   a. What adventures did Peter have in the snow?

   b. Have you done some of the things that Peter did?

   c. How would you spend your day in the snow?

   d. What happened to the snowball Peter put in his pocket?

2. Point out the art techniques used in the illustrations. Show the children how paint can be applied with a sponge to add background color.

3. Make a class *Big Book of Snowy Day Fun*. Have the children do the illustrations first. They can then write or dictate the text to accompany the pictures.

Special Feature
☐ Snowmen

1. In small groups, enjoy *The Snowman*, a wordless picture book by Raymond Briggs. Explore the illustrations and talk through the story with the children. Have them imagine what it would be like to have a snowman come to life. What things would they like to do together? What do they think the snowman would enjoy?

2. Read *Bob the Snowman*, by Sylvia Loretan. When Bob turned into a puddle, he realized that snowmen should not go south for the winter.

   Provide copies of page 47 for each student. Direct them to draw a series of pictures that tell about either their adventures with a snowman or the journeys of a snowman, such as Bob.

3. People who seldom see snow think it's special. Read *Midnight Snowman*, by Caroline Feller Bauer. Ask the students how they would go about building a snowman. List their ideas on a chart. The students may refer to the list as they organize their instructions for a how-to manual. Younger children may draw pictures to show the steps.

Activities

1. When and where snow is available, divide the class into small groups to build snowmen.

2. When the snowmen are finished, use them to reinforce a lesson in measuring. Provide yardsticks and yarn, and let the students measure and record pertinent information about their snowmen.

   a. How tall is it?

   b. How wide is the smile?

   c. How long is the nose?

   d. How round is the head?

3. Later, have the students compare measurements with other groups. They may use this information to create word problems.

4. Instruct the students to create a story about the snowman they made.

40 Winter

Additional Activities

For a cut-paper winter scene, use the directions below.

1. Provide dark blue paper, construction paper scraps (light, bright colors and white), scissors, glue and a hole punch. Direct the students to create the scene by cutting out shapes to make people, houses, trees, snowmen and other wintry figures. They may use the hole punch to make snowflakes. Avoid too many small pieces. The pieces should be glued in place and set aside to dry.

2. Discuss with the students sounds that are heard only in the winter. Brainstorm a list of winter sounds. After the words and phrases are recorded on a chart, have the students select phrases to make lists of their own. Some students may wish to divide their lists into Sounds I Like to Hear and Sounds I Don't Like, or Quiet and Noisy Sounds.

Resources

Nonfiction

Branley, Franklyn. *Snow Is Falling.* New York: Thomas Y. Crowell, 1986.

Cole, Joanna. *Plants in Winter.* New York: Thomas Y. Crowell, 1973.

Maass, Robert. *When Winter Comes.* New York: Henry Holt and Company, 1993.

Selsam, Millicent. *Where Do They Go? Insects in Winter.* New York: Four Winds Press, 1982.

Simon, Seymour. *Winter Across America.* New York: Hyperion Books for Children, 1994.

Fiction

Bauer, Caroline Feller. *Midnight Snowman.* New York: Atheneum, 1987.

Brett, Jan. *The Mitten.* New York: G.P. Putnam's Sons, 1989.

Briggs, Raymond. *The Snowman.* New York: Random House, 1978.

George, Jean Craighead. *Dear Rebecca, Winter Is Here.* HarperCollins, 1993.

Keats, Ezra Jack. *The Snowy Day.* New York: Viking Press, 1962.

Loretan, Sylvia. *Bob the Snowman.* New York: Viking, 1988.

San Souci, Daniel. *North Country Night.* New York: Doubleday, 1990.

Selsam, Millicent, and Joyce Hunt. *Keep Looking.* New York: Macmillan Publishing Company, 1989.

Tresselt, Alvin. *The Mitten.* New York: Lothrop, Lee & Shepard, 1964.

Winter Vocabulary Match

Draw a line connecting each word with the correct picture.
Color the pictures.

evergreen

icicles

snowflake

Plants in Winter

Seeds

Some plants go to seed in the fall. The seeds have tough covers that protect them from the cold. Warm weather makes the seeds grow.

Roots

In winter the stems and roots of dandelions are hidden away under the ground. In the spring new plants will grow from the stems.

Bulbs

If you plant a tulip bulb in the fall, it will rest all winter. In the spring look for green shoots and leaves to appear and then the flower.

Animals in Winter

Migration

Geese and other birds migrate when winter comes. They fly south to find food and warmer weather.

Hibernation

Chipmunks sleep through the winter. Their temperature drops. Their heartbeat and breathing slow down.

Adaptation

Animals in milder climates do not migrate or hibernate. There is less food. They are not as active during the shorter days.

The Mitten: Animal Characters

mole

hedgehog

rabbit

bear

owl

badger

fox

mouse

Who Am I?

Answer each riddle below with one of the animals on the right.

1. I have shiny teeth.

   Who am I? I am a _____.   rabbit

2. I have big kickers.

   Who am I? I am a _____.   hedgehog

3. I have glinty talons.

   Who am I? I am an _____.   fox

4. I have sharp prickles.

   Who am I? I am a _____.   owl

Write one more animal riddle. It doesn't have to be about an animal from the story.

I have _____.

Who am I?

I am a _____.

In the box below, draw a picture of your animal.

Name _____

Winter Clip Art

Winter Clip Art

Winter Clip Art

Winter Clip Art

Spring

Do You Know?

Why do plants begin to grow again in the spring?

Why are the animals so busy in the spring?

Teacher Background

The vernal equinox, which occurs on or about March 20, marks the start of spring. On this day, as Earth continues its trip around the sun, night and day are of equal length. Winter storms are forgotten. The warming climate coaxes plants and animals to become active once again. Sap rises in the trees and seeds begin to sprout underground. Hibernating animals stir and awaken from their winter sleep. Soon the countryside is alive with new life. Trees flower and leaf. Baby animals are born and hatch. Butterflies emerge from their protective chrysalises. Migrating birds and animals return from their winter homes and scurry to build nests and find food.

Information

You'll know when spring has arrived when the air grows warmer. The winter cover of snow melts slowly making way for sprouting plants of green. The sun rises earlier and sets later. Wildflowers add dots of color to grass-covered hills. Sap rises and fruit trees begin to bud. Blossoms form, bringing a promise of the fruit that is to come. Swelling leaf buds open. Tender new leaves appear and cover bare branches. Insects hatch from eggs and grow quickly as they nibble on leaves. Spiders spin webs and wait for prey to fly into their traps. Birds returning from winter homes swoop down to capture tasty bugs. Their songs fill the air as they stake out their territory. Nests will be built, hidden in the leafy branches. Eggs will be laid and kept warm and protected. When they hatch, the parents will be busy bringing food to hungry young hatchlings. At the pond, frogs lay jelly-like eggs. Returning ducks find hidden spots among the reeds to build their nests. Turtles, buried in the mud all winter, swim about looking for food. On the farm, farmers plow their fields preparing them for seeds they will sow. Crops already in the ground begin to appear as shoots poke out of the earth. Baby animals are born. Lambs and calves test spindly legs in pastures. Piglets squirm in warm mud. Newly hatched chicks hunt for bugs. Spring has arrived.

Talk About

What are some signs of spring?

What do you like best about spring? Is there anything you dislike?

——— Words to Know ———

blossom   chrysalis   hatchlings

Use the reproducible on page 63 to reinforce these vocabulary words.

Weather Watch

☐ Wind

Wind is moving air. In the spring, as the days grow warmer, air rises and cooler air rushes in to take its place. We can feel it, but we can't see it. We know the wind is blowing when tree branches dance and kites soar and plunge. We can tell from what direction it's blowing by wetting a finger and holding it in the air. The wind is coming from the side that feels colder.

Read and Enjoy

There are several wind-related poems and stories. Following are three to read and discuss with the students.

1. "Who Has Seen the Wind?" by Christina Rossetti.

    a. Talk about other ways you can tell the wind is blowing.

    b. Direct the children to draw pictures showing the wind at work.

2. *Gilberto and the Wind*, by Marie Hall Ets.

    a. Have the children talk about experiences they have had in the wind.

    b. Name some things the wind blew in the story. Take the students outside on a windy day. What objects do they see being blown by the wind?

    c. Have the students draw pictures similar to those in the book, using white chalk on tan paper.

3. Read *Windsongs and Rainbows*, by Albert Burton. The wind blows, signaling an approaching rainstorm. Hear, feel and see the wind, rain and sun. Have the students model the format, using their senses to describe the wind in a local setting.

Activities

1. Show the children how to make a wind sock. The streamers will show the direction from which the wind is blowing. Have them form a cylinder with a 4¹/₂" x 12" (11 x 30 cm) piece of construction paper. Glue crepe paper streamers to one end. Punch evenly spaced holes at the other. Attach four lengths of yarn and tie them together at the top. Hang the wind sock where it will catch the wind.

Materials
1 square sheet of paper
scissors
pencil with an eraser
paper clip

Directions

2. Make pinwheels with the children so they can test the wind's strength.

    a. Fold a square sheet of paper in half diagonally.

    b. Open and fold diagonally in the other direction.

    c. Cut along the creases from each corner to ¹/₂" (1.25 cm) from where the creases cross.

    d. Bend one corner of each section to the center and secure with an unfolded paper clip inserted in the eraser.

    Have the students hold the pinwheels in front of them and face the direction from which the wind is blowing.

3. Make simple paper airplanes. Experiment by flying them into the wind. What difference did it make in their flight?

Special Feature

Kites

Because of the early spring winds, March is a good time to fly kites.

1. Talk about kites and kite flying with the students. Have them share their experiences.

54 Spring

2. Discuss the following reminders with the students:
   a. Fly your kite in an open area away from wires.
   b. Never fly your kite in the rain, especially during a lightning storm.
   c. Keep your kite away from trees.
   d. Don't fly your kite near streets or roads.

   After the above suggestions have been discussed, ask the students for other reminders to add to the list.

3. Ask students the following questions to encourage them to think creatively:
   a. Imagine you are a kite, flying in the sky. How does it feel to be tossed by the wind?
   b. Would you rather be a kite or a paper airplane? Explain why you made your choice.

Plants

Growing Seeds

Plants grow from seeds. Seeds that were scattered in the fall are ready to start to grow in the spring. The sun warms the soil and signals the seeds to send out shoots. Roots grow deeper in the soil. Stems reach toward the sun.

Activities

Give the children the experience of growing plants from seeds by letting them experiment with birdseed.

Materials
Styrofoam™ cups
potting soil
gravel
birdseed

Directions

1. Make a small hole in the bottom of the cup and add gravel for drainage.
2. Add potting soil to within 1" (2.5 cm) of the top of the cup.
3. Sprinkle the seeds on the soil and then add more soil to cover them.

Put the cups on cookie sheets and place where the plants will receive sunlight. The soil should be kept moist.

A garden journal may be kept to record the plant's growth. Once shoots appear, the students may measure the plants and make sketches to show changes. Remind them to date each entry.

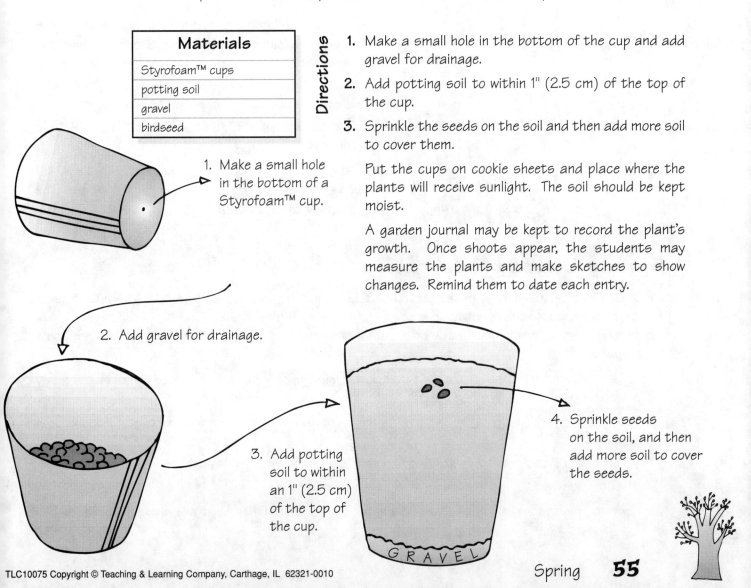

1. Make a small hole in the bottom of a Styrofoam™ cup.

2. Add gravel for drainage.

3. Add potting soil to within an 1" (2.5 cm) of the top of the cup.

4. Sprinkle seeds on the soil, and then add more soil to cover the seeds.

GRAVEL

Trees

☐ Rising Sap

The warmer days of spring signal the sap to rise from the tree roots. Sap is a sticky substance made of water and food for the tree. Leaf buds begin to open as sap spreads upward through the trunk. The students may wonder how the sap gets from the roots underground to the leaves on the branches.

Discovery Experiences

☐ Celery

Use a stalk of celery to demonstrate how sap flows through a tree. Begin this experiment early in the day so the colored water will have time to be drawn through the stalk.

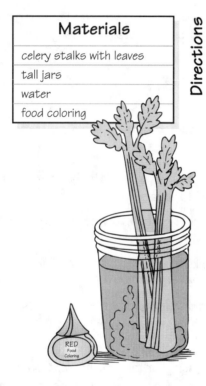

Materials
celery stalks with leaves
tall jars
water
food coloring

Directions

1. Pour the water into the jar and add several drops of food coloring.

2. Cut off about 1" (2.5 cm) from the bottom of the stalk of celery.

3. Place the stalk in the jar of water with the leaves up.

Have the children observe the color change as the colored water moves through the celery. Point out the location of the tubes visible at the end of the stalk. These appear as small dots along the outer edge. Just as the colored water moved up through the celery stalk, sap flows just beneath the bark of the tree.

In late winter and early spring, sugar maple trees are tapped to reach the sap flowing beneath the bark. The sap is boiled to remove most of the water. Maple syrup remains.

☐ Spring Holiday Celebration

Arbor Day is observed in most of the United States sometime during the spring. It is a day set aside to plant trees and to appreciate the many benefits we gain from them. Find out when Arbor Day is celebrated in your community. If possible, plan a tree-planting ceremony in which the children could participate.

To prepare, select from the list of activities below. Help the children become more aware of the many ways trees are used.

1. Read *Be a Friend to Trees*, by Patricia Lauber. Find out why trees are important to people and animals.

   a. List on a chart how trees are used by people and animals.

   b. Discuss ways to use less paper and save more trees.

2. Recycle magazines. Cut out pictures to make a collage of things that are made from trees.

Special Feature

☐ Spring Apple Trees

In the spring apple tree leaves appear first, then blossoms. The flowers are pink at first, then fade to white. Bees are attracted to the sweet smell of the apple blossoms. When they come to gather pollen and nectar, they pollinate the tree. Now there will be apples in the fall.

Activities

Materials
small squares of pink and white tissue paper
glue
crayons or paint for the truck and branches
pencil
paper

Directions

1. If the students have observed an apple tree first-hand, have them describe how it looked and smelled. Help them to use comparisons in their description.

   The tree looked like exploding popcorn.

2. To make a 3-D blossoming apple tree, follow the directions below.

   a. Color or paint the spreading branches of an apple tree. The trunk and limbs should cover much of the paper.

   b. Make blossoms for the tree. Place a square piece of tissue on the top of a pencil and twist it around the eraser. While it is still on the pencil, dip it into the glue and place it on a tree limb.

Insects

Butterflies lay eggs hidden from sight on the under parts of leaves. Young caterpillars eat their way out of the eggs. They eat leaves on the plant, grow out of their skins, shed them and eat some more. After growing through several skins, they molt for the last time. Attached to a leaf, the new skin hardens into a chrysalis. Inside the chrysalis many changes take place. When the time is right, it splits open to reveal a butterfly. This process is called metamorphosis.

1. Imagine with the students how it must feel to change from a caterpillar into a butterfly. Read *Where Butterflies Grow*, by Joanne Ryder.

2. Distribute copies of "A Magical Change" on page 64. Look at the pictures, read the captions and review the stages in the life cycle of a butterfly. Have the children color the page.

3. After studying metamorphosis, have the children pretend to crawl like a caterpillar and soar like a butterfly.

Birds

Birds are busy in the spring. They build nests, lay eggs and feed their young when they hatch. When looking for a nest site, birds are interested in three things—a safe place, materials to build the nest and a supply of nearby food.

Each type of bird builds a unique nest. Some are made of twigs and grass. Others are constructed of mud. Ducks build their nests on the ground hidden in reeds. Robins lay blue eggs in nests built high in tree branches.

Once the nest is built, the female lays eggs. She will sit on the nest keeping the eggs warm until the birds inside are ready to hatch. Both parents are kept busy feeding their young until they are strong enough to fly from the nest.

Activities

1. To reinforce bird activity in spring, distribute copies of page 65 to each student.

   Depending on their age and ability, select one of the following activities for them to complete:
   a. Color the pictures and talk about what is happening in each.
   b. Color, cut out and glue the pictures in order on another sheet of paper. Captions may be written or dictated.
   c. Assemble a *Birds in Spring* booklet. Glue one picture on each page. Briefly write to tell what is happening. Design a cover for the booklet.

2. Divide the class into small groups to write a report. Assign each group one local bird to study. Provide reference materials and pictures. Instruct the students to observe the bird firsthand while it is flying, feeding and at rest. They should notice its size, colors and markings. Encourage them to ask questions of their own that could lead to further investigation. They can then read to find answers to their questions and find out more about the bird.

3. If possible, get an incubator and fertilized chicken eggs for your classroom. The eggs take 21 days to hatch.

   You can tell when an egg is ready. A small hole begins to appear as the chick uses its egg tooth to break the shell. You may hear peeping.

   When the chick is out of the shell, it should remain in the incubator until it is dry and fluffy. Then it may be moved to a box warmed with a 60-watt light bulb. It will eat cornmeal and will need water. Before beginning the project, be sure the chicks will have homes after they are hatched.

58   Spring

Special Feature

☐ Eggs

Birds aren't the only egg layers. Reptiles, amphibians, insects and even some mammals also lay eggs. Following is a brief description of turtles, frogs and spiders that hatch from eggs.

Turtles

The mother turtle digs a hole in the ground, lays her leathery eggs and covers them with soil. She leaves and does not return. The eggs are kept warm by the sun. The newly hatched turtles dig their way to the surface.

Frogs

When ponds are free of ice, frogs lay clumps of jelly-coated eggs on the surface of the water. Tadpoles hatch from the eggs. They slowly develop from small fish-like creatures to adult frogs, that swim in the water and hop about on land.

Spiders

In the fall a spider lays hundreds of eggs that are protected through the winter in a cocoon. When the weather grows warmer, spiderlings, that look like small adult spiders, hatch from the eggs. When they begin to nibble on each other, it is time for them to spin their own webs.

Distribute copies of page 66. The top section briefly summarizes information about the turtles, frog and spider. The bottom half requires the students to imagine what might be inside the egg pictured. They may write a description of what they think is in it and draw a picture in the egg.

Literature Connection

Rechenka's Eggs, by Patricia Polacco.

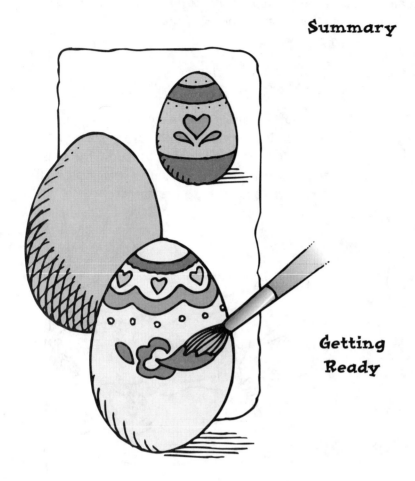

Summary

All winter Babushka painted beautiful eggs to take to the Easter festival. One day she rescued a goose that had been shot by a hunter. She named her Rechenka and cared for her.

When Rechenka recovered, she accidentally tipped over the basket breaking all of the special eggs. For the next 13 mornings, Babushka found a wonderfully decorated egg in the goose's basket. She was able to go to the festival where she won first place.

Babushka knew the goose would leave soon to join her flock, but she didn't expect the gift that Rechenka left behind.

Getting Ready

The story takes place in the Ukraine, a part of Russia. Explain that the clothing, food and buildings pictured reflect the culture of the Ukrainian people. Artists paint eggs like the ones shown in the book. The miracles that Babushka referred to are special things that happen unexpectedly.

Reading the Story

Read to find out how two near misfortunes turned into two special events. Allow extra time for viewing the illustration.

Thinking About the Story

1. Name two things that happened in the story that could have turned out badly but did not.

2. What did the old woman and the goose do to avoid disaster? Which character in the story do you think was kinder? Why?

3. How did Rechenka's eggs compare to Babushka's?

4. Should Babushka have told her friends about the goose's eggs? Should she have accepted the prize?

5. How was the egg Rechenka left different than the other ones she laid?

6. Do you think the gosling will grow up to lay painted eggs?

7. Which events in the story could really happen? Which were make-believe?

1. Have the students use felt-tipped markers to decorate the egg on page 67. They may fill the space using the shapes of sun, moon and stars, flowers, leaves and other designs.

2. To make a mosaic using eggshells, you will need about two eggshells for each student, cardboard (no larger than 6" x 6" [15 x 15 cm]), glue and watercolors.

   Direct the students to:

   a. Draw a simple outline of an object of their choice—fish, animal, egg.

   b. Break the shells into smaller pieces.

   c. Spread glue on one area of the figure and sprinkle on the shells.

   d. Press the shells in place and apply glue to another area.

   e. Paint the mosaic figure with watercolors when the glue has dried.

Animals

Many animals are born in the spring. They grow quickly as the days become warmer. Calves, foals and lambs drink milk from their mothers. When they are a little older they will feed in grassy pastures. Ducklings and goslings nibble on tender shoots along lakes and ponds.

1. Share pictures of farm animals with the children. Discuss why spring is a good time for animals to be born.

2. Distribute copies of page 68. Have the children match the baby with the parents in the animal family. They may draw a picture to illustrate their idea of springtime on a farm.

Signs of Spring

The following activities will help summarize the spring theme:

1. Write an acrostic poem to describe spring. Have the students write the word *spring* vertically on the left side of the page. Use the letters to begin each line of the poem. Words, phrases or sentences, telling about the season, may be used to complete the lines.

2. Brainstorm a list of phrases to describe the sights and sounds of spring. Write the responses on a chart. Give each student two 6" x 9" (15 x 23 cm) pieces of white or light-colored construction paper.

   Direct them to:
   a. Fold the sheets of paper in half to form a booklet.
   b. Select four phrases from the chart they think best describe spring.
   c. Write one phrase on each page and draw a picture to accompany it.
   d. Provide samples of wallpaper for the cover. Staple the pages together and give the book a title.

Resources

Nonfiction

Beer, Kathleen Costello. *What Happens in the Spring?* Washington, D.C.: National Geographic Society, 1977.

Brown, Craig. *In the Spring.* New York: Greenwillow Books, 1994.

Heller, Ruth. *Chickens Aren't the Only Ones.* New York: Grossett & Dunlap, Inc., 1981.

Hirschi, Ron. *Spring.* New York: Cobblehill Books, 1990.

Lauber, Patricia. *Be a Friend to Trees.* New York: HarperCollins Publishers, 1994.

Maass, Robert. *When Spring Comes.* New York: Henry Holt and Company, 1994.

Markle, Sandra. *Exploring Spring.* New York: Atheneum, 1990.

Schweninger, Ann. *Springtime.* New York: Viking, 1993.

Selsam, Millicent, and Joyce Hunt. *A First Look at Bird Nests.* New York: Walker and Company, 1987.

Selsam, Millicent, and Joyce Hunt. *A First Look at Caterpillars.* New York: Walker and Company, 1987.

Fiction

Burton, Albert. *Windsongs and Rainbows.* New York: Simon & Schuster for Young Readers, 1993.

Butterfield, Moira. *Bird.* New York: Simon & Schuster, 1992.

Ets, Marie Hall. *Gilberto and the Wind.* New York: Viking Press, 1963.

Polacco, Patricia. *Chicken Sunday.* New York: Philomel Books, 1992.

Polacco, Patricia. *Rechenka's Eggs.* New York: Philomel Books, 1988.

Ryder, Joanne. *Where Butterflies Grow.* New York: Lodestar Books, 1989.

Poetry

Rossetti, Christina, "Who Has Seen the Wind?" in *Sing a Song of Popcorn.* New York: Scholastic Inc., 1988.

Spring Vocabulary Match

Draw a line connecting each word with the correct picture.
Color the pictures.

chrysalis

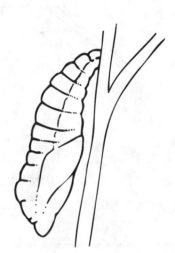

hatchlings

blossom

Name _____

A Magical Change

Eggs

Eggs are hidden on the
underside of leaves.

Caterpillar

Caterpillars eat leaves and grow.

Chrysalis

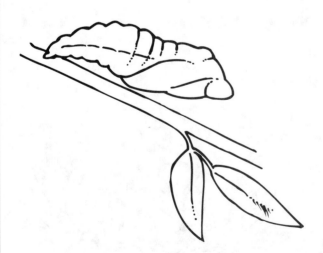

A caterpillar's last skin hardens
to form a chrysalis.

Butterfly

The chrysalis splits open
and a butterfly appears.

Name _____

Birds in Spring

Name _____

Eggs in Spring

	Turtle	Frog	Spider
Eggs	Leathery	Jelly-coated	Tiny
Laid In	Ground	Water	Silk cocoon
Young	Turtle	Tadpole	Spiderling

What is inside the egg?

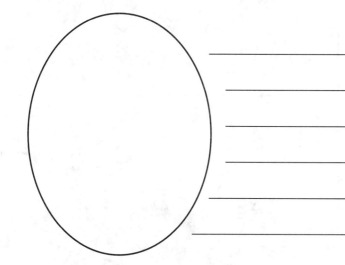

_____

_____

_____

_____

_____

_____

Name _____

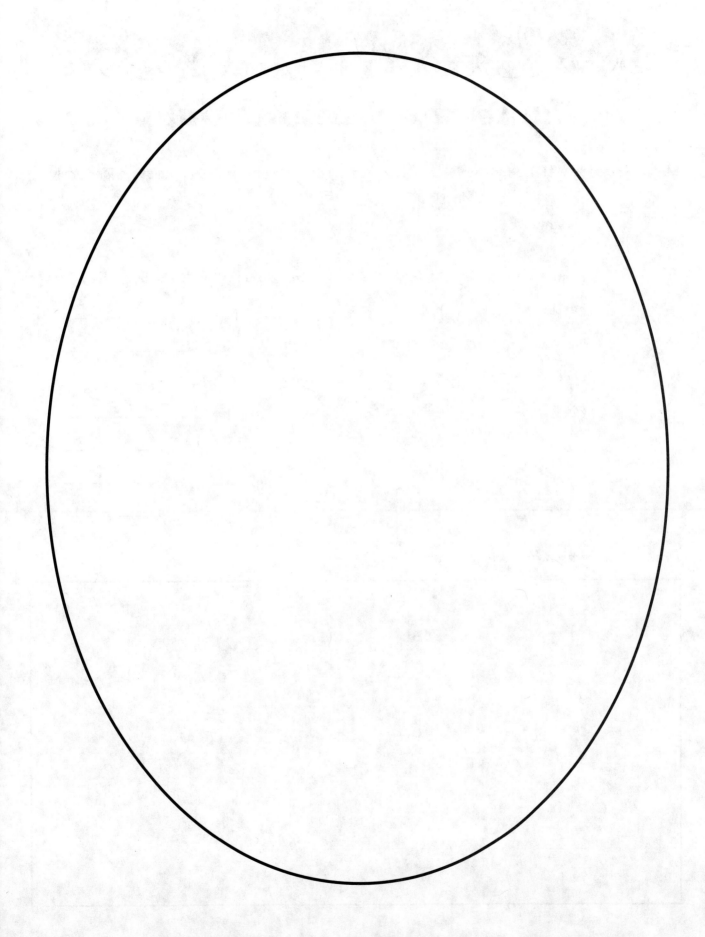

Name _____

Name the Animal Baby

Match the baby with its mother and father. Write the correct word to complete each family.

foal   duckling   calf   piglet

lamb   gosling   chick

Family	Male	Female	Baby
cattle	bull	cow	_____
chicken	rooster	hen	_____
sheep	ram	ewe	_____
geese	gander	goose	_____
pig	boar	sow	_____
duck	drake	duck	_____
horse	stallion	mare	_____

Draw a picture below of springtime on a farm.

TLC10075 Copyright © Teaching & Learning Company, Carthage, IL 62321-0010

Spring Clip Art

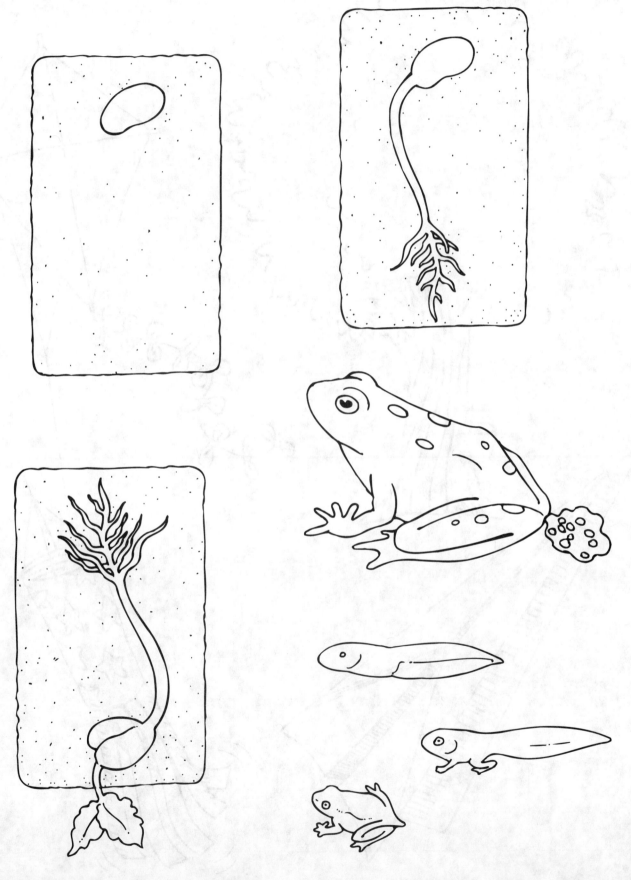

Spring Clip Art

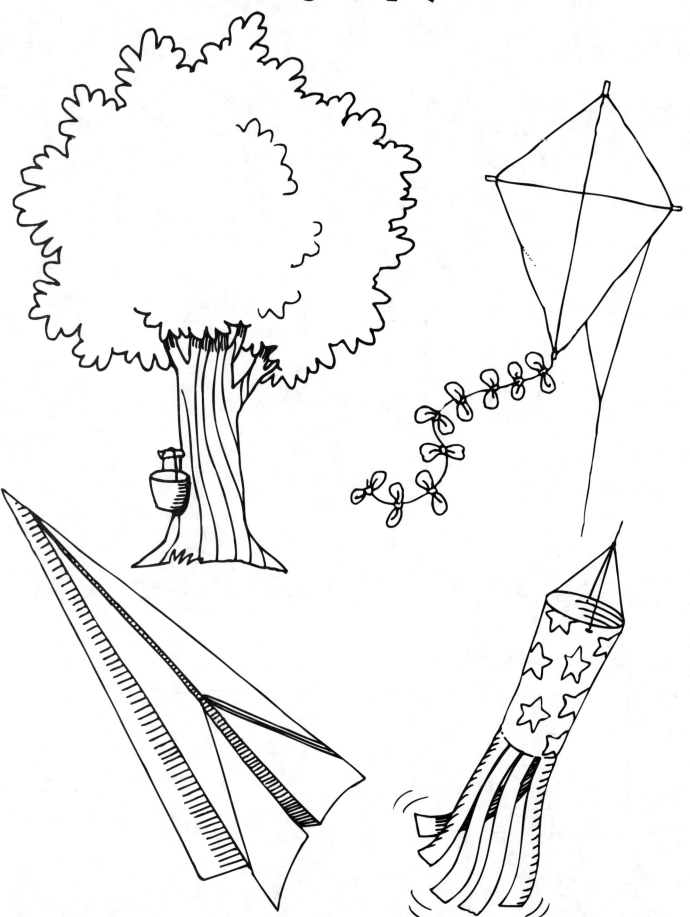

Spring Clip Art

Spring Clip Art

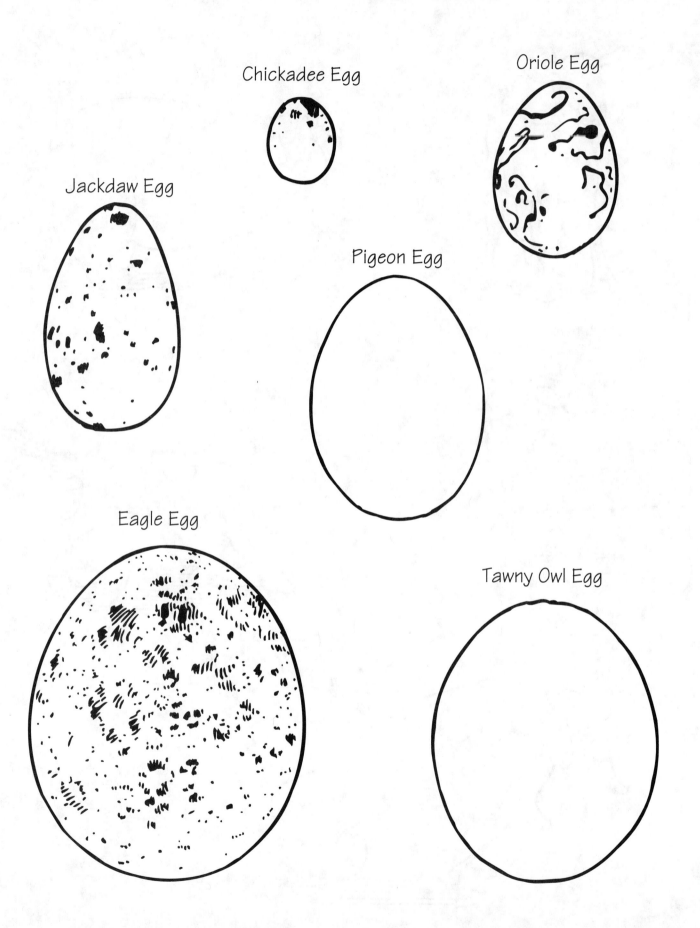

Chickadee Egg

Oriole Egg

Jackdaw Egg

Pigeon Egg

Eagle Egg

Tawny Owl Egg

Summer

Do You Know?

Why is it warmer in the summer?

What are some signs of summer?

CROAK
CROAK
CROAK

Teacher Background

The summer solstice marks the beginning of summer. The longest day of the year falls on June 21. In the Northern Hemisphere, because of the angle of the Earth, the sun's rays strike the Earth's surface more directly. The more intense heat and longer daylight hours mean higher temperatures. From now until the beginning of winter, there will be a little less sunlight each day. The rush of spring is over. Young animals grow and learn. Fruits and vegetables ripen; flowers bloom. The hums, buzzes and chirps of insects fill the air.

Plants use the extra summer sunshine to grow more quickly. Birds and animals seek the shade of leafy branches on hot summer days. A fine mist of water released from the leaves helps to cool the air.

Student Information

You will know it is summer when the days are longer and hotter. Everything is growing everywhere. Peaches, apricots and cherries ripen on the trees. Vegetable gardens keep salad bowls full and weeders busy. Flowers bloom and bees buzz as they gather nectar and pollen.

Insects are everywhere. There are enough to feed birds, spiders and frogs. There are plenty to visit picnics and to bite people when they least expect it.

You will know it is summer when the night air is warm and crickets chirp and frogs croak. Fireflies signal with their flashing lights. You many even have to go to bed before it is dark.

Summer is the time to be outdoors. It is picnic and barbecue time. Days may be spent at the beach or park. It is fun to swim and dive in the lake or pool. Hours of running and racing are followed by resting and reading under leafy branches.

As in other seasons, there is work to do, games to play and things to discover, but in the summer it seems like more fun. The sights and sounds of summer fill our eyes and ears with memories.

Talk About

How can you tell summer has begun?

What do you like best about summer? Is there anything you don't like?

Words to Know

cirrus   cumulus   stratus

Use the reproducible on page 86 to reinforce these vocabulary words.

Weather Watch

☐ Clouds

Clouds form when water evaporates. The heat from the sun makes water evaporate, turn into vapor and disappear in the air. Vapor rises into the sky where it cools and turns into clouds of tiny droplets.

There are three main types of clouds. Cirrus clouds are high in the sky. They are made of ice crystals. Some people call them mares' tails because of their wispy appearance. Rain may be on the way.

Cumulus clouds are big and puffy. They don't usually produce rain. These are the clouds to watch as they change shapes and tease the imagination.

Stratus clouds are usually low and cover the whole sky like a blanket. These may produce a drizzle or light rain.

These main cloud types combine to give us a variety of weather conditions. To learn more about clouds, read *The Cloud Book*, by Tomie de Paola.

Have the students use white crayons on white paper to show different types of clouds. When they cover the entire page with a wash of thin blue tempera, the waxed clouds will resist the paint and show up against the sky blue paint.

Discovery Experience
☐ How Clouds Form

Demonstrate how clouds form in the sky. This is best shown to small groups, so they can observe the experiment close up. You will need a jar one-third full of warm water, a small plastic bag of ice, one sheet of black paper and matches (for adults only).

1. Light the match and hold it briefly over the opening of the jar. Drop it into the jar. Cover the opening with a bag of ice.

2. Place the black paper behind the jar so the students will be able to see the cloud forming. Water droplets will also appear on the inside of the jar.

3. Explain that when the warm water rises it is cooled and droplets form. The smoke from the match gives the water particles something to attach to.

Activities

1. On a day when the sky is full of cumulus clouds, read *It Looked Like Spilt Milk*, by Charles G. Shaw. Have the children help identify the shapes as the story is read.

2. Take the students outside. Find a comfortable spot and watch the clouds float overhead. What shapes do you see? Can anyone see the same things?

3. Start a Clouds Look Like chart. Brainstorm a list of imaginative phrases to describe clouds.

   Sample: like piles of whipped cream

4. Begin a class book based on *It Looked Like Spilt Milk*. Give everyone a sheet of 9" x 12" (23 x 30 cm) blue paper and a copy of page 87. Have the students cut out the rectangle holding the sentence frames. They may use the rest of the paper to carefully tear out a cloud. They should study it from all directions to decide what it resembles. Glue the completed sentence to the left-hand side of the blue paper. The cloud goes on the right side.

   Note: Instead of torn paper, use cotton balls. Have the students gently pull on the cotton to spread it out. When attaching it, they should spread a little glue on the paper with their finger before placing the cloud on top.

Plants

Fruit, vegetables and flowers grow quickly during the summer months. Colorful plants appear in many gardens and parks.

1. Read *Eating the Alphabet*, by Lois Ehlert. Some fruits and vegetables will be familiar to everyone, others may not. A glossary provides helpful and interesting information about each item shown.

   a. Challenge the children to think of produce that was not mentioned.

   b. Discuss the importance of including fruits and vegetables in a healthy diet. What are their favorite fruit snacks? What vegetables do they like?

   c. Have the students write directions for cooking a vegetable of their choice. They should include at least three steps.

   d. Ask the children to bring in pieces of fruit to use as models for a mural painting. Review the colorful art in *Eating the Alphabet*. Remind them to make their drawings large.

   e. When the art is completed, cut up some of the fruit and serve in a fruit salad with flavored yogurt for dressing, or thread it on wooden skewers for fruit kabobs.

2. Make a list of colorful produce and flowers. How many different kinds of fruit are orange? How many vegetables are red? Name some yellow flowers.

3. Set up a chart to organize the students' responses. Focus on their needs. You may change the color words or specialize in just fruits or vegetables.

	Red	Yellow	Orange
Vegetable			
Fruit			
Flower			

4. Make a class ABC book, *Plants from A to Z*. Assign one letter to each child. Direct them to look through seed catalogs to find plants with names that begin with their letter. The pictures may be arranged on the pages and the completed pages bound into a book.

5. Direct the students to cut out pictures from seed catalogs to make color collages.

Trees

Plants can produce their own food by a process called photosynthesis. Chlorophyll is a pigment in leaves that makes them green. Because of the chlorophyll, leaves are able to use energy from the sun, water from the soil and carbon dioxide in the air to produce sugar and oxygen. The plants use the sugar to grow. We breathe the oxygen.

Read and Enjoy

1. Read *A Tree Is Nice*, by Janice Udry. Talk about what makes a tree nice. Have the children name things that were mentioned in the book and add others.

   Direct them to fold a sheet of paper into four parts. They may select four things to draw that show what they like about trees. Have them put a star by the one they think is the most important.

   a. Name some birds and animals that depend on trees for food.

   b. What animals use trees for shelter?

2. Learn how trees provide food and shelter for all types of wildlife. Read *Crinkleroot's Guide to Knowing the Trees*, by Jim Arnosky.

3. Read *The Giving Tree*, by Shel Silverstein. The tree in the story is an apple tree, but all trees are "giving."

   a. What did the tree in the story give the boy?

   b. What do other types of trees have to offer?

   c. Discuss how trees are grown to provide fruits, nuts and other products we use every day.

Special Feature
☐ Summer Apple Trees

The apples are growing. Green plants make their own food. Sunlight, air and water combine with the chlorophyll in the leaves to make the apples grow bigger and sweeter. When summer comes to an end, the apples will ripen and be ready to eat. While the apples are developing, new buds are forming. They will be next year's leaves and flowers.

Activities

1. Cut an apple in half beginning at the stem end, so students can study the core.

2. Distribute copies of page 88 to the students. The pictures show views of the inside of an apple, as well as a blossom and a bee, the main pollinator. Direct the students to color and cut out the parts of the apple mobile. To give the pieces more body, mount them on construction paper and cut out leaving a margin of color. Attach the mobile pieces to a wire coat hanger or twig with heavy thread or yarn.

Insects

Insects have six legs and three body parts (head, thorax and abdomen). Most insects have wings. During the summer, insects can be seen and heard everywhere. Some are helpful. Bees make honey. Ladybugs eat aphids that hurt plants. Other insects are pests. Many chew leaves. Mosquitoes bite people. Plan a field trip to see insects in action. You can find them almost everywhere.

Note: *Bugs*, by Nancy Winslow Parker and Joan Richards Wright, presents a fascinating way to introduce the study of insects to children.

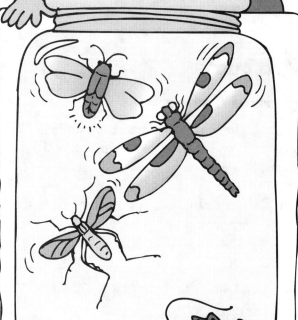

Discovery Experience
☐ Insect Study

Insects are all around us, but we seldom take the time to look at them closely. These activities will give the students an opportunity to notice details and make comparisons.

1. Before beginning the search, collect jars with holes punched in the lids for catching bugs, nets to capture flying insects and hand lenses for close up viewing. Once outside, look for insects crawling on and under leaves, hiding under logs, rocks or flowerpots, and flying through the air.

2. After a bug is captured, observe how many legs and body parts it has. Does it have wings? What color is it? Encourage the students to take notes to aid their memories.

3. Direct the students to write a short report about one of the insects they observed and include a drawing of it. They may use the questions in #2 as a guide, or they may fill in the responses on the form on page 89.

4. Have the students imagine what it would feel like to be an insect crawling on the ground. Give them the opportunity to explore a grassy area. What do leaves look like from below? How tall would a blade of grass seem to a tiny insect? Direct the students to draw a bug's-eye view of the area.

5. Challenge the students to recycle "junk" to create a bug of their own design. Egg cartons, pipe cleaners, paper scraps, paint, colored markers and various odds and ends can be used to create.

6. When finished, have the "entomologists" tell something about their completed insects. What kind of bug is it? Where can it be found? What does it eat? Does it harm or help plants and people?

Special Feature

☐ Fireflies

Read Fireflies! by Julie Brinckloe. Ask if they think the boy in the story did the right thing at the end when he released the fireflies. Have the children tell about firsthand experiences they have had catching fireflies in jars. Have they ever felt like the boy in the story?

1. Have them think of words and phrases that would help someone who has never seen a firefly imagine what it would look like.

2. If the children have never been around fireflies, ask what they think they look like?

Explain that fireflies are signaling to attract a mate. Although magical in the dark of night, they are actually small brown insects in the daylight.

Birds

There is plenty of food for growing birds in summer. You can guess what a bird eats by looking at its beak. Meat eaters, like owls, have strong, hooked beaks. Wrens and other insect eaters have thin beaks to pick bugs from the ground. Finches have short cone-shaped beaks to crack seeds. Hummingbirds have long thin bills to reach nectar in flowers. Herons stand quietly in shallow water, waiting for a fish to grasp with their long thin beaks.

1. Distribute copies of page 90. Study the types of beaks; then have the students answer the riddles.

2. Can the students name other birds that are meat, insect, seed, nectar or fish eaters? Have them make up riddles about these birds.

3. Distribute copies of page 91. Instruct the students to color and cut out the body of the bird and the box for the wings. Mount the bird on construction paper or tagboard to make it sturdier. The wings should be accordion pleated and folded in half. The children will need help making the slit for the wings.

Animals

Animals settle down after the excitement of spring. Young animals grow quickly during the warm summer months. Wild animals learn to hunt or hide from hunters. Food is easiest to find this time of year.

People

During the summer months, when the weather is warmer, there are many things to do outdoors. Sometimes the children have to be reminded of what is available.

1. Copy and distribute page 92. Go over the items on the list. Invite the students to add their own special activities.

2. Have them number their favorite activities from one to five or ten—one being the favorite. Tally the results. Which activity received the most votes? Which came in second and third?

3. Have the students tell or write about one summer activity they enjoy. They should explain why they like it.

Literature Connection

Three Days on a River in a Red Canoe, by Vera B. Williams.

Summary A young girl tells of a trip on a river with her cousin, aunt and mother. The children learned new things and enjoyed being outdoors for three days.

Getting Ready If you were going to take a trip in a canoe, what would you pack? Suppose you were going to be gone for three days?

Reading the Story As the students listen, have them put themselves in the place of the children in the story. Imagine how it would feel out on the river and camping along the shore.

Thinking About the Story

1. Name some things they learned to do. What was the most important?
2. What was the best part of the trip for them?
3. What was the most frightening?
4. What part would they not want to do again?
5. What surprised them the most?
6. If you had been there, what part would you have liked?
7. What did they learn to cook?
8. If you have been camping, did your family fix something special to eat?

Activities

1. Have the children think of an imaginary place they could visit. Direct them to:
   a. Sketch a map of the area. They could refer to the maps in the book.
   b. Talk about the things they would see and the activities they could do.
   c. Write the journal-like entries, telling about what they did as they traveled from place to place.
   d. Draw pictures to accompany the writing. The pictures should show themselves and what they saw during the trip.
   e. Combine the writing and pictures to make a book.
2. People send postcards telling about their trip to their friends and relatives. Have the students make their own postcards on 4" x 6" (10 x 15 cm) cards. Direct them to draw a picture on one side showing the place they are visiting. On the other side they may write a message and address the card.

Special Feature
☐ Outings

Summer is a time to spend outdoors. Often there is more time to do the things we like to do. The weather is fine and the days are longer. Following are ideas for three trips.

A Day at the Beach

A walk along the beach will turn up twisted pieces of driftwood, colorful stones and a variety of seashells. Tide pools hold sea animals caught at high tide awaiting the return of the sea at the next high tide. Seabirds fly overhead and dart along the water's edge in search of food.

Arrange a trip to the beach. If this is not possible, plan beach-related activities with shells and water-smoothed stones. Talk about and share pictures of tide pool animals.

Materials

Materials
large sheets of paper (two for each student)
tempera
colored markers
scissors
stapler
newspaper for stuffing

Directions

1. Collect water-smoothed stones from along the beach. If you plan to paint them, wash them with soap and water when you get home. Before beginning to paint, have the children study the stone to see what the shape suggests to them. They can decide whether to completely cover the surface with paint or to just add color to accent some parts. They may wish to leave the stone unpainted, but brush on a coat of acrylic sealer. This will make the stone glossy and bring out its natural colors.

2. Have the students create giant, stuffed paper fish. Since fish come in many shapes, sizes and colors, they may use their imaginations freely.

   Direct the students to:

   a. Draw a large fish outline on a sheet of paper.

   b. Paint colorful designs to give the fish a one-of-a-kind appearance.

   c. Cut out the fish, place it facedown on a second piece of paper and trace around the outline.

   d. Paint the second fish shape, which is the back. A solid color is fine.

   e. Place the two unpainted sides together and begin to staple the tail sections together.

   f. Crumple pieces of newspaper to fill the fish.

   g. Continue to staple the edges as paper is added.

At the Beach

This is what I like the most!
Sandy beaches at the coast,
Driftwood fires, warm as toast,
Cooling breezes, I won't roast.
An outing at the beach!
Is this what you like the most?
A trip to the sandy coast,
Tasty hot dogs, set to roast,
Fluffy marshmallows to toast.
A picnic at the beach!

by Patricia O'Brein

A Trip to the Zoo

A zoo is a place where you can visit animals you might not be able to see otherwise. Many people are involved in taking care of these animals. In *Zoo*, by Gail Gibbons, readers go behind the scenes. There is much more to a zoo than the animals in the exhibits. Read this or a similar book to the children.

1. Name some animals you would see at a zoo.

2. Have students select one animal to feature on a poster. Include a caption, pictures and information about the animal.

3. As a follow-up to a trip to the zoo, or instead of a zoo outing, have the children create a zoo with animal cookies. Give each student a cookie to trace. Direct them to trace around the outside, add features and color in the shape. They may then include a background setting. Beneath the picture, have them write or dictate a few lines about the animal.

The Circus Comes to Town

The circus comes to town in the summer. To capture the feeling of excitement, read *If I Ran the Circus*, by Dr. Seuss. Some companies parade the animals in decorated cages from the train to the place where they will perform. Make circus parade wagons to display in the classroom.

Materials

Styrofoam™ meat trays
paper to fit the bottom of the trays
tagboard for wheels
crayons
felt-tipped pens
yarn
blunt large-eye needles
glue

Directions

1. Have the children draw real or imaginary animals to put into the circus wagon.

2. Glue the paper to the inside bottom of the tray.

3. With the needle, punch holes about 1" (2.5 cm) apart along the top and bottom edges.

4. Thread the yarn through the holes to make "bars."

5. Trace around a circle template to make wheels for the wagon.

Read and Enjoy

1. Read *A Summer Day*, by Douglas Florian. A family takes a trip to the country. The entire day is described in groups of two- or three-word phrases. Discuss things the students could do on summer days. Make a list of short phrases recording their ideas.

   Have each student fold a 6" x 18" (15 x 46 cm) strip of construction paper into four parts and then refold it to make an accordion book. Direct them to give their book a title. They may then write and illustrate four phrases they feel capture his or her summer day.

2. In *The Goodbye Walk*, by Joanne Ryder, a child says good-bye to the places she visited on her vacation. Read the story and have the students share similar experiences they have had.

Signs of Summer

1. Write the following sentences on cards and place in a pocket chart:

Fish jump.	Kids laugh.
Flowers bloom.	Stars twinkle.
Corn ripens.	Mice hide.
Owls hoot.	Weeds grow.
Water splashes.	Flies hum.
Frogs leap.	Bees buzz.
Clouds form.	Kids fish.
Fireflies glow.	Rain falls.

   Have the students:

   a. Compose more two-word sentences.

   b. Suggest ways to group the sentences into categories.

      (sights, sounds, weather, animals, insects)

   c. Expand the sentences with prepositional phrases, first orally and then written.

      Sample: Stars twinkle in the sky.

2. Direct the students to select at least four sentences to include in a *Signs of Summer* booklet. Have them write one sentence on each page; then draw a picture to illustrate it. Staple the completed pages together inside a decorated cover.

84 Summer

Resources

Nonfiction

Allison, Linda. *The Sierra Club Summer Book.* Boston: Little Brown and Company, 1977.

Arnosky, Jim. *Crinkleroot's Guide to Knowing the Trees.* New York: Bradbury Press, 1992.

Brandt, Keith. *What Makes It Rain?* Mahwah, NJ: Troll Associates, 1982.

De Paola, Tomie. *The Cloud Book.* New York: Holiday House, Inc., 1975.

Gibbons, Gail. *Zoo.* New York: Thomas Y. Crowell, 1987.

Maass, Robert. *When Summer Comes.* New York: Henry Holt and Company, 1993.

Parker, Nancy Winslow, and Joan Richards Wright. *Bugs.* New York: Greenwillow Books, 1987.

Parker, Steve. *Insects.* Dorling Kindersley, Inc., 1992.

Thomson, Ruth. *Summer.* New York: Watts, 1990.

Fiction

Brinckloe, Julie. *Fireflies!* New York: Macmillan Publishing Company, 1985.

Ehlert, Lois. *Eating the Alphabet: Fruits and Vegetables from A to Z.* San Diego: Harcourt Brace Jovanovich, 1989.

Ehlert, Lois. *Growing Vegetable Soup.* San Diego: Harcourt Brace Jovanovich, 1987.

Florian, Douglas. *A Summer Day.* New York: Greenwillow Books, 1988.

Geisel, Theodor (Dr. Seuss). *If I Ran the Circus.* New York: Random House, 1956.

Ryder, Joanne. *The Goodbye Walk.* New York: Lodestar Books, 1993.

Shaw, Charles G. *It Looked Like Spilt Milk.* New York: HarperCollins Publishers, 1949.

Silverstein, Shel. *The Giving Tree.* New York: Harper & Row Publishers, 1964.

Stevenson, James. *July.* New York: Greenwillow Books, 1990.

Udry, Janice. *A Tree Is Nice.* New York: Harper & Row Publishers, 1956.

Williams, Vera B. *Three Days on a River in a Red Canoe.* New York:
Greenwillow Books, 1981.

Name _____

Summer Vocabulary Match

Draw a line connecting each word with the correct picture.

cirrus

cumulus

stratus

Clouds

Sometimes it looked like a _____,
but it wasn't a _____

Name _____

Apple Mobile

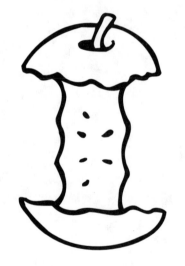

Name _____

My Insect Report

This is where I found the insect.

This _____

has _____ legs. It has _____ body parts.

It has/doesn't have wings.

Its color is _____.

This is how it looks.

Birds and Beaks

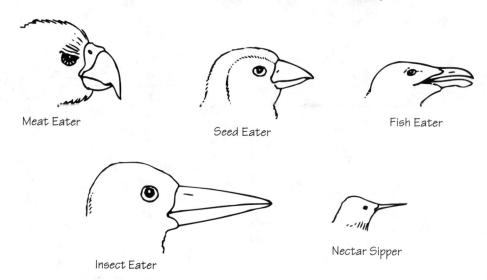

Meat Eater

Seed Eater

Fish Eater

Insect Eater

Nectar Sipper

What Am I?

Answer each riddle with the name of a bird.

I hunt for mice and rabbits. I use my hooked beak and feet like a knife and fork.

I am a _____.

I crack seeds open with my strong, short bill.

I am a _____.

I sip nectar from flowers with my long thin beak.

I am a _____.

I catch fish with my spear like beak.

I am a _____.

I eat insects. I catch them with my thin beak.

I am a _____.

Name _____

Name _____

Summer Fun for Everyone

Number your favorites. Begin with number one.

__ flowers to smell   __ trees to climb   __ fireworks to watch

__ weeds to pull   __ pools to swim   __ insects to collect

__ fish to catch   __ games to play   __ friends to visit

__ watermelon to eat   __ lemonade to sell   __ books to read

__ baseballs to hit   __ hills to climb   __ paths to follow

__ fireflies to chase   __ ice cream to enjoy   __ bikes to ride

__ _____

__ _____

__ _____

Draw a picture of something you like to do in the summer.

Summer Clip Art

Summer Clip Art

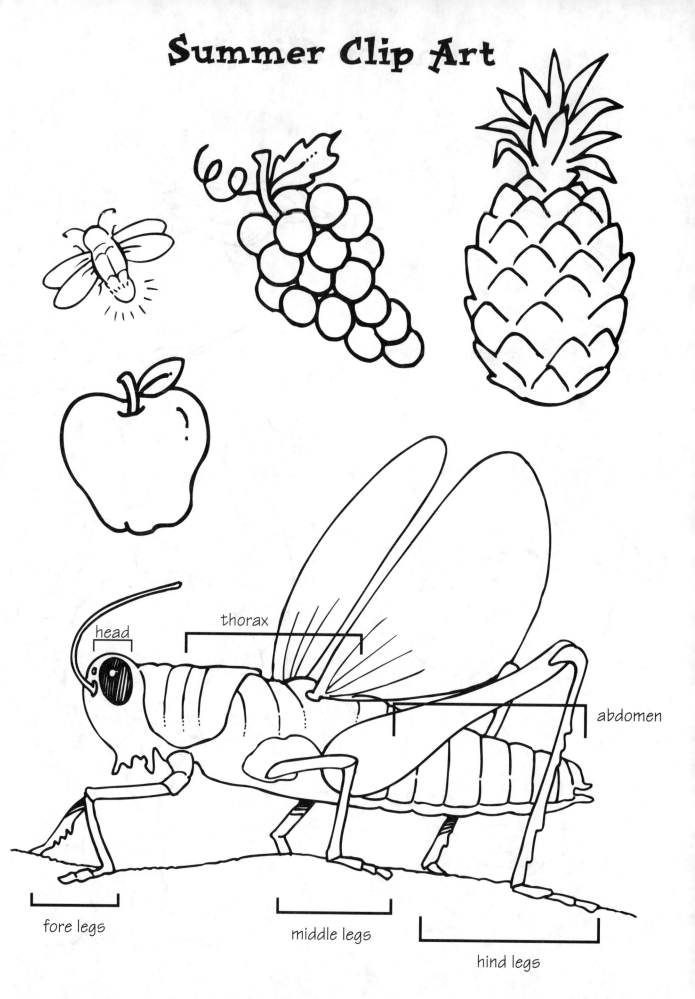

head

thorax

abdomen

fore legs

middle legs

hind legs

Summer Clip Art

Summer Clip Art

The Seasons

Day by Day

There are daily changes with each season. Local weather patterns differ from place to place.

1. Talk with the students about times the weather made them change their plans.

2. Discuss the water cycle in relation to changing weather conditions.

   a. Why do we need sun, clouds, rain and snow?

   b. What happens when there is too much or too little rain or snow?

   c. Review the role the sun plays in the amount of rain that falls.

   d. Distribute copies of page 104 for the students to complete.

3. Keep a weather chart to show changes during the week or month. As a part of the opening routine each morning, have students take turns recording local weather conditions. They may use the chart on page 105 to indicate precipitation, cloudiness, wind and temperature. A thermometer with a Fahrenheit and Celsius scale will be helpful.

Month by Month

1. Calendars are constant reminders of the passing year. Time is measured from holiday to holiday. Special events are noted and anticipated. Involve the students in a monthly calendar project. Make a calendar grid. Use yarn to divide the days and weeks on the bulletin board.

   a. Review holidays and events for the upcoming month. Include birthdays and local celebrations.

   b. Number 4" x 6" (10 x 15 cm) cards, one for each day of the month, and distribute to the students.

   c. Have students prepare a date for the upcoming month. They will decorate the cards, noting special days and events.

   d. Post their cards so they will be on display the entire month.

2. Read poems from *Chicken Soup with Rice*, by Maurice Sendek.

   a. Have the children copy and illustrate each month's poem throughout the year.

   b. They may learn the poems and recite them together.

Through-the-Year Literature Connection

Ox-Cart Man, by Donald Hall.

Summary

In the fall, the ox-cart man and his family filled the cart with things they made and grew during the year. He set off on foot for the market to sell everything. When he returned home, the family would again work through the year getting ready for market in the fall.

Getting Ready

The story takes place in the early 1800s. At that time farm families grew the food they needed and sold the rest. The money they earned was used to buy items they didn't produce on the farm. Help the children imagine what it would have been like living on a farm long ago.

Reading the Story

As the story is read, suggest the children study the illustrations to note the different seasons. Ask what clues they might look for that would show seasonal changes (plants, clothing, activities).

Thinking About the Story

1. What did the family pack into the cart in October?

2. What did the ox-cart man see on his way to and from Portsmouth market?

3. What did he see at the market? What did he buy?

4. How did the family spend their time during winter, spring and fall?

5. What do you think they did during summer?

6. What season do you think was their favorite? What did they like best about it?

7. What animals were mentioned? How did each one help the family?

Activities

1. Draw a map to show places on the farm, as you imagine them.

2. Distribute copies of page 106 to the students. Direct them to fold the paper in half lengthwise and cut along the lines to the center fold. The section underneath each flap may be illustrated to show seasonal changes or activities on the farm through the year.

☐ Anno's Counting Book

Anno's Counting Book, by Anno Mitsumasa, shows seasonal changes through the 12 months of the year. It provides numerous opportunities to count people, trees, birds, animals, flowers and buildings. Even children who are able to count well will enjoy using the book.

1. This book is best enjoyed by partners. The children can take turns counting things and asking each other questions about the illustrations. (What season is it? How can you tell? How many objects can be found and named that fit the number category? How do the pictures change from month to month? Which building is new in the picture? What kind of work is being done?)

2. Divide the class into small groups. Give each group a large sheet of butcher paper. They may pick a number and a season to feature in their drawings. Remind them that when working with a small number to think of many different things to draw. Many items from the same category will have to be drawn, if they choose a large number.

   Note: As an alternative, provide rubber stamps that may be used with felt-tipped pens and crayons to complete the pictures.

3. Compile a class counting book. Have the children who prefer working independently to do the pages with small numbers. Groups may work on the pages with large numbers.

4. The cover of Anno's Counting Book pictures one sun, two evergreen trees, three buildings and so on. Have the students make similar drawings with a seasonal theme including many different items to count. The completed drawings may be used for additional counting practice.

5. Use the book illustrations as a plot source for storytelling. Have the students tell or write a story about something that is happening in one of the pictures.

   Sample: In the picture, two children are chasing two rabbits. Will the children catch the rabbits? If the rabbits escape, how do they do it? What would you do if you were one of the children? Suppose you were one of the rabbits?

Writing Poetry
☐ The Diamante

The diamante is a poem of opposites. It begins with one topic and ends with its opposite. The seven lines are written in the shape of a diamond.

One word–topic 1 (noun)

Two words to describe topic 1 (adjectives)

Three words ending in -ing referring to topic 1 (participles)

Four words–two referring to topic 1, two to topic 2 (nouns)

Three words ending in -ing referring to topic 2 (participles)

Two words to describe topic 2 (adjectives)

One word–topic 2 (noun)

Sample:

Caterpillar

furry, fuzzy,

crawling, creeping, munching

Ground Creeper, Sky Flier

flitting, fluttering, sipping

light, airy,

Butterfly

Follow the steps below to write a group diamante.

1. Build a word bank for each line listing words on a chart for easy reference.

2. When the topic and its opposite have been established, brainstorm words for line two and its opposite, line six.

3. Select three words from each list that best describe line one and line seven. Write them in the poem.

4. Continue listing and choosing words for lines three and five, and line four.

5. Once the children understand the procedure, have them write their own poem, selecting words of their choice from the word bank.

Creating Diamante Poems

Work in small groups to write seasonal-related diamante poems. The students may select from the suggestions of opposites below or use their own ideas.

Spring–Fall   Winter–Summer   Hot–Cold   Rain–Snow

☐ The Couplet

A couplet is made up of two rhyming lines with the same rhythm.

1. The children listen to the couplets below and identify the season referred to in the lines.

   Ponds freeze.   Rain showers.   Leaves fall.
   Kids sneeze.   Wildflowers.   Geese call.
            Frogs leap.   Sleds glide.
            Birds peep.   Animals hide.

2. Have the students write original two line rhymes. They may create some about seasons or another topic of their choice.

3. Read "I Walk By," by Evelyn Beyer. It uses couplets to describe how several animals move.

   a. As the poem is read, the students may supply the rhyming words.

   b. Have the students demonstrate how they would move like each animal mentioned in the poem.

   c. Present the poem as a choral reading.

☐ The Concrete Poem

Splish Splash is a book of poetry to listen to and look at. Introduce the students to the fun of concrete poems, where images are created with words. Water—from raindrop to ocean is the topic. Pick a seasonal theme and let the children experiment making pictures with words.

Additional Activities

1. Following are suggestions students may use to complete page 107. Have them use the center circle to highlight the theme of the page. They may complete it using words or pictures.

   a. Picture yourself doing something you like to do during each season.

   b. Feature sports or games you play during the year.

   c. Picture the same scene as it would look at different times during the year.

   d. If a specific tree has been observed through the year, make sketches of it as it appears each season.

   e. Picture seasonal outdoor activities.

   f. Show the stages of an insect from egg, larva, pupa to adult.

2. Write the words from the word search on page 108 on tagboard. Place them in a pocket chart and review with the children. When they have become familiar with the words, distribute copies of page 108. After the words have been located in the puzzle, they may complete the rest of the page and make up other categories.

Resources

Nonfiction

Arnosky, Jim. *Crinkleroot's Guide to Knowing the Birds*. New York: Bradbury Press, 1992.

Arnosky, Jim. *Crinkleroot's 25 Birds Every Child Should Know*. New York: Bradbury Press, 1993.

Berger, Melvin. *Season*. New York: Doubleday, 1990.

Busch, Phyllis. *Backyard Safaris: 52 Year-Round Science Adventures*. New York: Simon & Schuster Books for Young Readers, 1995.

Gibbons, Gail. *The Reasons for Seasons*. New York: Holiday House, 1995

Gibbons, Gail. *The Seasons of Arnold's Apple Tree*. San Diego: Harcourt Brace, 1994.

Gibbons, Gail. *Weather Words*. New York: Holiday House, 1990.

Goennel, Heidi. *Seasons*. Boston: Little Brown and Company, 1986.

Lambert, David. *The Seasons*. New York: Watts, 1983.

Lauber, Patricia. *Be a Friend to a Tree*. HarperCollins Publishers, 1994.

Fiction

Anno, Mitsumasa. *Anno's Counting Book*. New York: HarperCollins Publishers, 1977.

Borden, Louise. *Caps, Hats, Socks, and Mittens*. New York: Scholastic Inc., 1989.

Gantschev, Ivan. *Good Morning, Good Night*. Saxonville, MA: Picture Book Studios, 1991.

Griffin, Sandra Ure. *Earth Circles*. New York: Walker and Company, 1989.

Hall, Donald. *Ox-Cart Man*. New York: Viking, 1979.

Lesser, Carolyn. *What a Wonderful Day to Be a Cow*. New York: Alfred A. Knopf, 1995.

Pearson, Susan. *My Favorite Time of Year*. New York: Harper & Row, 1988.

Provensen, Alice and Martin. *A Year at Maple Hill Farm*. New York: Aladdin Paperbacks, 1988.

Rockwell, Anne. *First Comes Spring*. New York: Thomas Y. Crowell, 1985.

Rockwell, Anne. *Our Yard Is Full of Birds*. New York: Macmillan Publishing Company, 1992.

Zolotow, Charlotte, *Summer Is . . . .* New York: Thomas Y. Crowell, 1983.

Poetry

Beyer, Evelyn. "Jump or Jiggle," in *Read Aloud Rhymes for the Very Young*. New York: Alfred A. Knopf Books for Young Readers, 1986.

De Reginers, Beatrice Schenk. *Sing a Song of Popcorn*. New York: Scholastic Inc., 1988.

Graham, Joan Bransfield. *Splish Splash*. New York: Fields Books for Young Readers, 1994.

Hopkins, Lee Bennett. *The Sky Is Full of Song*. New York: Harper & Row, 1983.

Livingston, Myra Cohn. *A Circle of Seasons*. New York: Holiday House, 1982.

Prelutsky, Jack. "The Four Seasons," in *The Random House Book of Poetry for Children*. New York: Random House, 1983.

Prelutsky, Jack. *The Random House Book of Poetry for Children*. New York: Random House, 1983.

Prelutsky, Jack. *Read-Aloud Rhymes for the Very Young*. New York: Alfred A. Knopf, 1986.

Sendek, Maurice. *Chicken Soup with Rice*. New York: Harper & Row, 1962.

Seasonal Activities

Warm sun shines on the water.	The water evaporates.
Clouds form overhead.	Rain or snow falls from the clouds.

Name _____

Weather Chart

	Day 1	Day 2	Day 3	Day 4	Day 5
Precipitation					
Sky					
Wind					
Temperature					

Precipitation			Sky			Wind			Temperature	
Rain	Snow		Clear	Partly Cloudy	Cloudy	Calm	Breezy		Fahrenheit	Celsius

Spring	Summer	Fall	Winter

Name _____

Seasonal Activities

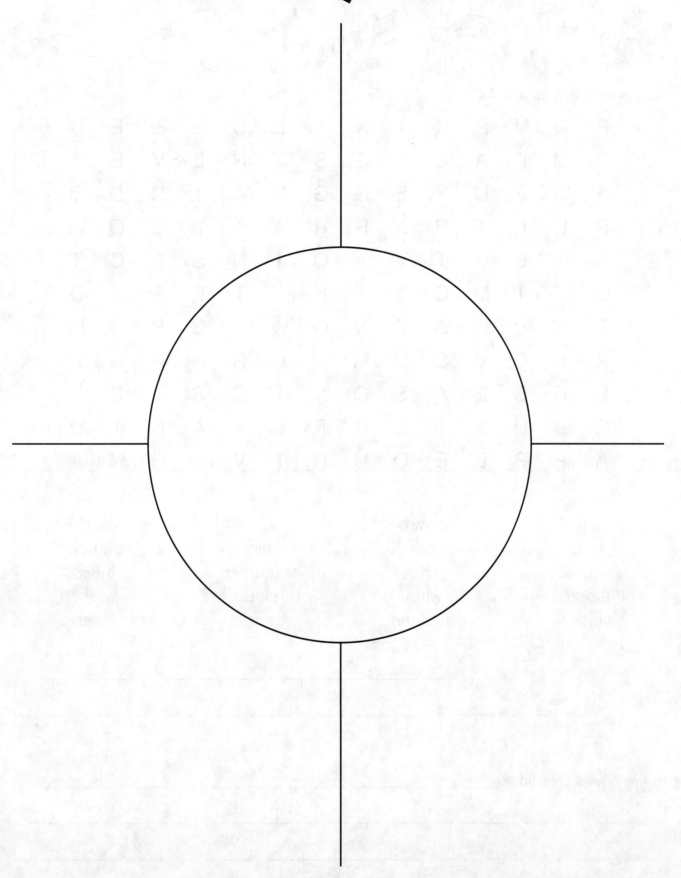

Name _____

Seasonal Word Search

Look across and up and down.

```
P U M P K I N T L C S E E D
C M F A L L G S T H L V B I
A W J U Y E G G N W I N D O
R E L T R A R R A I N B O W
R A B U T V A Q I N S E C T
O T I M C E I K I T E S L D
T H R N W S N O W E S P O M
X E D V S U M M E R H R U L
E R S E A S O N T D S I D F
G B U T T E R F L Y A N T U
A P P L E O U R T V B G N A
```

spring	snow	seed	egg
ant	leaves	apple	weather
rain	fall	bird	pumpkin
rainbow	kite	summer	insect
butterfly	wind	cloud	season
winter	autumn	carrot	wet

Find things that can fly. _____ _____

_____ _____ _____

Name things that grow. _____ _____

_____ _____ _____

_____ _____ _____

An Apple Tree Through the Year

Spring	Summer
Leaves and blossoms cover the branches. Bees visit the tree.	Small apples begin to grow among the green leaves.
Fall	Winter
The fruit is ripe. It's time to pick the apples.	The branches are bare. Winter has come.

Seasonal Clip Art

Seasonal Clip Art

Seasonal Clip Art

Seasonal Activities